Daily
Academic Vocabulary

GRADE 6

Editorial
Development: Bonnie Brook
Communications
Content Editing: Marilyn Evans
Leslie Sorg
Copy Editing: Cathy Harber
Art Direction: Cheryl Puckett
Cover Design: Cheryl Puckett
Illustration: Jim Palmer
Design/Production: Carolina Caird
Arynne Elfenbein

EMC 2762

Evan-Moor®
Helping Children Learn

Visit
teaching-standards.com
to view a correlation
of this book.
This is a free service.

**Correlated to
Current Standards**

**Congratulations on your purchase of some of the
finest teaching materials in the world.**

For information about other Evan-Moor products, call 1-800-777-4362,
fax 1-800-777-4332, or visit our website, www.evan-moor.com.
Entire contents © 2007 EVAN-MOOR CORP.
18 Lower Ragsdale Drive, Monterey, CA 93940-5746. Printed in USA.

CPSIA: Printed by McNaughton & Gunn, Saline, MI USA. [1/2018]

Contents

Daily Academic Vocabulary • EMC 2762 • © Evan-Moor Corp.

About Academic Vocabulary

What Is Academic Vocabulary?

Academic vocabulary is that critical vocabulary that students meet again and again in their reading and classroom work across all content areas. Feldman and Kinsella refer to these high-use, widely applicable words—words such as *compare*, *occurrence*, *structure*, *sequential*, *symbolize*, and *inference*—as "academic tool kit words."[1]

Why Is Academic Vocabulary Instruction Important?

Vocabulary knowledge is one of the most reliable predictors of academic success. Studies show a major difference over time between the achievement levels of children who enter school with a strong oral vocabulary and those who begin their schooling with a limited vocabulary. Dr. Anita Archer says, "In many ways the 'Reading Gap,' especially after second and third grades, is essentially a Vocabulary Gap—and the longer students are in school the wider the gap becomes."[2] Focused vocabulary instruction can reduce this gap.

Knowing academic vocabulary—the "vocabulary of learning"—is essential for students to understand concepts presented in school. Yet academic English is not typically part of students' natural language and must be taught. "One of the most crucial services that teachers can provide, particularly for students who do not come from academically advantaged backgrounds, is systematic instruction in important academic terms."[3]

What Does Research Say About Vocabulary Instruction?

Common practices for teaching vocabulary—looking up words in the dictionary, drawing meaning from context, and impromptu instruction—are important but cannot be depended upon alone to develop the language students need for academic success.

Most vocabulary experts recommend a comprehensive vocabulary development program with direct instruction of important words. *Daily Academic Vocabulary* utilizes direct teaching in which students use academic language in speaking, listening, reading, and writing. Used consistently, *Daily Academic Vocabulary* will help students acquire the robust vocabulary necessary for academic success.

[1]Feldman, K., and Kinsella, K. "Narrowing the Language Gap: The Case for Explicit Vocabulary Instruction." New York: Scholastic, 2004.

[2]Archer, A. "Vocabulary Development." Working paper, 2003. (http://www.fcoe.net/ela/pdf/Anita%20Archer031.pdf)

[3]Marzano, R. J. and Pickering, D. J. *Building Academic Vocabulary*. Alexandria, VA: Association for Supervision and Curriculum Development, 2005.

Tips for Successful Vocabulary Teaching

The "Weekly Walk-Through" on pages 6 and 7 presents a suggested instructional path for teaching the words in *Daily Academic Vocabulary*. Here are some ideas from vocabulary experts to ensure that students get the most from these daily lessons.*

Active Participation Techniques

- Active participation means ALL students are speaking and writing.

- Use **choral responses**:
    - Pronounce the word together.
    - Read the sentence/question together.
    - Complete cloze sentences together.

- Use **nonverbal responses**:
    - Students give thumbs-up signal, point to the word, etc.
    - Make sure students wait for your signal to respond.

- Use **partner responses**:
    - Have students practice with a partner first.
    - Listen in on several pairs.

- Allow thinking time before taking responses.

- Randomly call on students; don't ask for raised hands.

- Ask students to rephrase what a partner or other classmate said.

Model and Practice

- Use an oral cloze strategy when discussing a new word. Invite choral responses. For example: *If I read you the end of a story, I am reading you the ___.* (Students say, "conclusion.")

- Complete the open-ended sentence (activity 1 on Days 1–4) yourself before asking students to do so.

- Make a point of using the week's words in your conversation and instruction (both oral and written). Be sure to call students' attention to the words and confirm understanding in each new context.

- Encourage students to look for the week's words as they read content area texts.

- Find moments during the day (waiting in line, in between lessons) to give students additional opportunities to interact with the words. For example:

    *If what I say is an example of **accomplish**, say "accomplish." If what I say is <u>not</u> an example of **accomplish**, show me a thumbs-down sign.*

    > *I meant to clean my room, but I watched TV instead.* (thumbs down)
    > *Stacia read two books a week, more than any other student.* ("accomplish")
    > *The scientists found a cure for the disease.* ("accomplish")
    > *The mechanic could not fix our car.* (thumbs down)

* See also page 9 for specific ideas for English language learners.

Each week of *Daily Academic Vocabulary* follows the same five-day format, making the content more accessible for both students and teacher.

Using the reproducible definitions and the teacher lesson plan page, follow the instructional steps below to introduce each day's word or words.

1. **Pronounce** the word and point out the part of speech. Then have students say the word with you several times. If the word is long, pronounce it again by syllables, having students repeat after you.

2. **Read the definition** of the word; paraphrase using simpler or different language if necessary.

3. **Read the example sentence** and then have students read it with you. Discuss how the word is used in the sentence and ask questions to confirm understanding. For example: *We are waiting for a **definite** answer from Aunt Caitlin about when she is coming for a visit.* Ask: *What kind of answer would be a **definite** answer? What kind of answer would <u>not</u> be a **definite** answer?* Provide additional example sentences as necessary.

4. **Elaborate** on the meaning of the word using the suggestions on the teacher lesson plan page. These suggestions draw on common life experiences to illustrate the word meaning and give students opportunities to generate their own examples of use.

Teacher Resources

Reproducible Definitions

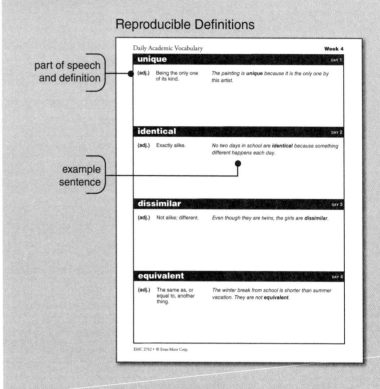

Teacher Lesson Plan

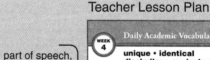

from *Daily Academic Vocabulary*, Grade 6, EMC 2762

Student Practice Pages

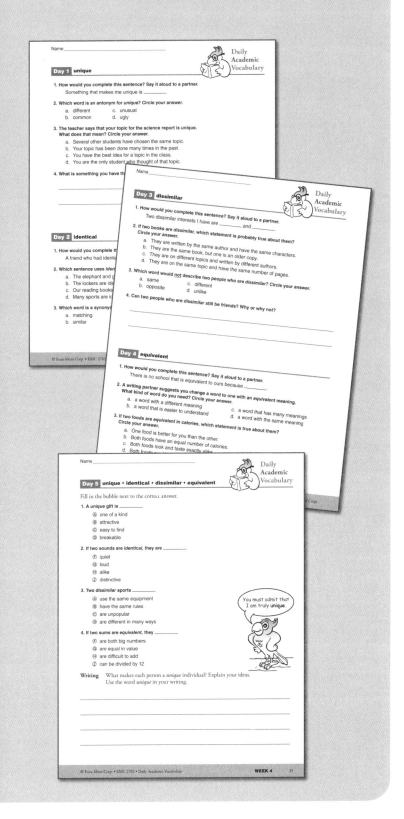

5. **Assess** students' understanding of the word(s) with the reproducible activities for Days 1 through 4.

The first item is always an oral activity that is designed to be open-ended and answerable based on personal experience. You may wish to model a response before asking students to complete the item. Make sure that all students respond orally. Then call on a number of students to share their responses or those of a partner.

Until students become familiar with the variety of formats used in the daily practice, you may wish to do the activities together as a class. This will provide support for English language learners and struggling readers.

6. **Review and assess** mastery of all the words from the week on Day 5. The review contains four multiple-choice items and a writing activity requiring students to use one or more of the week's words.

The instructional steps above were modeled after those presented by Kevin Feldman, Ed.D. and Kate Kinsella, Ed.D. in "Narrowing the Language Gap: The Case for Explicit Vocabulary Instruction," Scholastic Inc., 2004.

Review Week Walk-Through

Weeks 9, 18, 27, and 36 are review weeks. Each review covers all the words from the previous eight weeks.

Days 1–4

On Day 1 through Day 4 of the review weeks, students determine which academic vocabulary words complete a cloze paragraph.

Day 5

Day 5 of the review weeks alternates between a crossword puzzle and a crack-the-code puzzle.

Teacher Page

alphabetical list of the words to be reviewed

suggestions for ways to conduct review lessons

Extension ideas suggest ways to tie the words into subject area content.

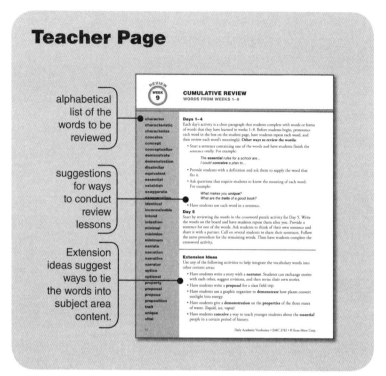

Student Practice Pages

Days 1–4

Day 5

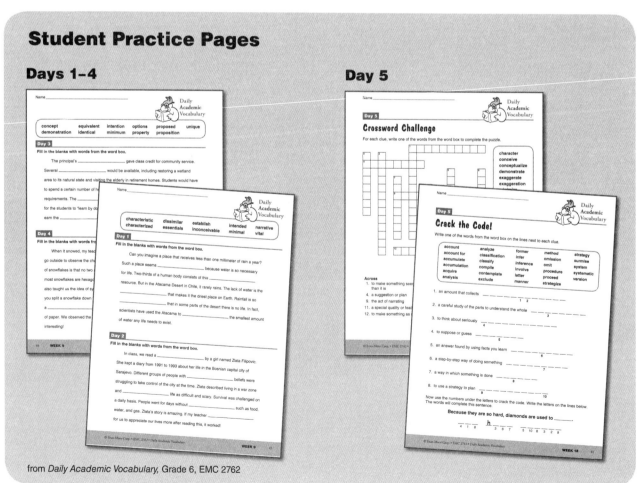

from *Daily Academic Vocabulary*, Grade 6, EMC 2762

Meeting the Needs of English Language Learners

In addition to the direct, scaffolded instruction presented in *Daily Academic Vocabulary,* you may want to use some of the following sheltering strategies to assist English language learners in accessing the vocabulary.

Use Graphics
Draw a picture, a symbol, or other graphics such as word or idea maps to represent the word. Keep it simple. Then ask students to draw their own pictures. For example:

categorize   similar

Use Cognates with Spanish-Speaking Students
Cognates—words that are similar in meaning, spelling, and pronunciation—can make English more accessible for Spanish speakers. There are thousands of English words that have a related Spanish word. For example:

typical	típico
variety	variedad
combination	combinación

Model Correct Syntax and Usage in Oral Discussions
Model correct pronunciation. Use echoing strategies to teach correct usage and syntax. Teach the varied forms of words together, *agree* and *agreement* for example, to help students understand correct usage.

Provide Sentence Frames
For written activities, such as the final activity on all Day 5 pages, provide sentence starters or sentence frames that students can complete. For example:

*We knew that our study method was **effective** because…*

Teach Communication Strategies
Engaging in academic discussions requires a more formal language. Teach a variety of ways to begin responses when reporting or asking questions in class. For example:

Change this	To this
My partner said…	My partner shared/pointed out/indicated that…
That's not right!	I don't agree with you because…
I don't get it.	Will you explain that to me again?

conceive • inconceivable
concept • conceptualize

Use the reproducible definitions on page 160 and the suggestions on page 6 to introduce the words for each day.

DAY 1

conceive
(verb) To think up or form in the mind. *Kari will **conceive** a plan to raise money for the new theater.*

Say: *I **conceive** lesson plans each day to help you learn. I think them up in my mind. Have you ever **conceived** the plot of a story or an experiment for a science fair?* Point out that **conceiving** an idea or plan often involves creative thinking. Then have students complete the Day 1 activities on page 11. You may want to do the first one as a group.

DAY 2

inconceivable
(adj.) Impossible to believe or imagine. *It was **inconceivable** to me that Luis would not tell the truth.*

Write on the board "in = not" and "able = capable of." Say: *Yesterday we learned that "conceive" means "to think of or imagine an idea." Using the meanings of the prefix and suffix I've written, what do you think **inconceivable** means?* Help students put the meanings together. ("not capable of imagining") Ask: *What are things you would describe as **inconceivable**?* Then have students complete the Day 2 activities on page 11. You may want to do the first one as a group.

DAY 3

concept
(noun) A general idea or thought. *Fairness is a **concept** that most people understand.*

Have students give a few examples of idea nouns (e.g., truth; democracy), and write them on the board. Say: *Another word for "idea" is **concept**. A **concept** is a "big" or general idea, such as "fairness" in the sample sentence.* Ask: *What are other "big idea" **concepts**?* (e.g., justice; peace) Then have students complete the Day 3 activities on page 12. You may want to do the first one as a group.

DAY 4

conceptualize
(verb) To form a concept or idea. *When inventors **conceptualize** solutions to problems, they create new inventions.*

Say: *"Conceive" and **conceptualize** are synonyms.* Ask: *What base word do you see in the word **conceptualize**?* (concept) *How can you use the word "concept" to help define the verb **conceptualize**?* (Students should connect the word with ideas and action.) Say: *Like "conceive," **conceptualize** describes the mental activity, or thinking, involved in forming or creating ideas. It is what you do when you think of a concept. What are some situations at school when you might be asked to **conceptualize**?* Have students complete the Day 4 activities on page 12. You may want to do the first one as a group.

DAY 5

Have students complete page 13. Call on students to read aloud their answers to the writing activity.

Day 1 conceive

1. How would you complete this sentence? Say it aloud to a partner.

I would like to conceive a way to _____.

2. Which word is a synonym for *conceive*? Circle your answer.

a. express

b. discover

c. think

d. build

3. Which skill or quality would help you *conceive* an idea for a science fair project? Circle your answer.

a. creative thinking

b. neat handwriting

c. good manners

d. a strong sense of smell

4. Describe a plan or idea you *conceived* with your friends.

_____

_____

Day 2 inconceivable

1. How would you complete this sentence? Say it aloud to a partner.

It would be inconceivable to ask a friend to _____.

2. Which word is an antonym for *inconceivable*? Circle your answer.

a. impossible

b. believable

c. unthinkable

d. incredible

3. Imagine a writing assignment where you are asked to create a fantasy character. List three qualities or physical traits that would make the character seem *inconceivable*.

a. _____

b. _____

c. _____

Day 3 concept

1. How would you complete this sentence? Say it aloud to a partner.

A concept I find hard to understand is _____.

2. Which sentence does <u>not</u> use *concept* correctly? Circle your answer.

   a. Matt understands the concept of energy.
   b. Angela's concept of fun is anything to do with sports.
   c. We discussed several concepts in science class.
   d. You can concept gravity by dropping an object.

3. Which word does <u>not</u> fit the usual *concept* of friendship? Circle your answer.

   a. respect   c. honesty
   b. loyalty   d. selfishness

4. Do you understand the *concept* of academic vocabulary? What is it?

_____

_____

Day 4 conceptualize

1. How would you complete this sentence? Say it aloud to a partner.

A job that might require being able to conceptualize is _____.

2. Imagine you were working to *conceptualize* a new invention. Which step would <u>not</u> be a logical part of the process? Circle your answer.

   a. You come up with an idea in your mind.
   b. You write the idea down on paper and try to work out the details.
   c. You look for the invention you need in a book or on the Internet.
   d. You see a need for a new invention.

3. Which of these would help you most when you need to *conceptualize* an idea? Circle your answer.

   a. being a clear thinker
   b. being a neat notetaker
   c. being a friendly person
   d. being a careful speller

Name_____

Day 5 conceive • inconceivable
concept • conceptualize

Fill in the bubble next to the correct answer.

1. Which of these is <u>not</u> something that a person could *conceive*?

Ⓐ a story plot

Ⓑ a game idea

Ⓒ an escape plan

Ⓓ a live animal

2. Which word is the best synonym for *inconceivable*?

Ⓕ unbelievable

Ⓖ unusual

Ⓗ odd

Ⓘ typical

3. Which noun names a *concept*?

Ⓐ college

Ⓑ knowledge

Ⓒ professor

Ⓓ computer

4. Which sentence uses the word *conceptualize* correctly?

Ⓕ Let's conceptualize our new friends after school.

Ⓖ We need time to conceptualize experience in science.

Ⓗ Sometimes it is easier to conceptualize a plan than to carry it out.

Ⓘ We were able to invent a new machine because we could not conceptualize.

Writing Describe your *concept* of the perfect school day. Use the word *concept* in your writing.

_____

_____

_____

_____

propose • proposal
proposition • intend • intention

Use the reproducible definitions on page 161 and the suggestions on page 6 to introduce the words for each day.

DAY 1

propose
(verb) To suggest a plan or idea to be considered. *Each member will propose a topic for the group project.*

proposal
(noun) A suggestion or plan. *The group wrote a proposal to take a field trip.*

Say: *When you propose something, you suggest it for others to think about, with the understanding that it may be accepted or rejected.* Ask: *Has anyone ever proposed an idea for an activity or a project to classmates? What was it?* Ask: *How might propose and proposal be related?* (e.g., a **proposal** is the idea that is **proposed**) Explain that a **proposal** can be a spoken suggestion or a written plan. Then have students complete the Day 1 activities on page 15. You may want to do the first one as a group.

DAY 2

proposition
(noun) An offered or suggested plan of action. *Enrique's proposition was that he would mow her lawn for a small fee.*

Ask: *How do you think "proposal" and proposition are alike?* (Both have "propose" as a base word.) Explain that the words are basically identical, but that a **proposition** is often more of an offer or deal than just an idea or suggestion. Say: *I have a proposition for you. If all of you ___, then I will ___.* (e.g., finish work; bring cookies) *Do you have a proposition for me?* Then have students complete the Day 2 activities on page 15. You may want to do the first one as a group.

DAY 3

intend
(verb) To have something in mind as a goal, plan, or purpose. *The students intend to raise money to pay for a class trip.*

Ask: *If you intend to get a good grade in this class, does that mean you have set a goal for yourself, or that you have already achieved it?* (set the goal) Explain that **intend** means to have something specific in mind that you want to do or achieve. Ask: *Do people always do what they intend to do? What do you intend to do today?* Then have students complete the Day 3 activities on page 16. You may want to do the first one as a group.

DAY 4

intention
(noun) Something that you mean to do. *The team's intention is to win the final game.*

Explain that "intend" and **intention** have a relationship that is similar to that of "propose" and "proposal" from Day 1. Say: *An intention is something that you intend, or mean, to do. It is my intention to teach you the meaning of intention. What is an intention you have for this week?* Then have students complete the Day 4 activities on page 16. You may want to do the first one as a group.

DAY 5

Have students complete page 17. Call on students to read aloud their answers to the writing activity.

 Daily Academic Vocabulary • EMC 2762 • © Evan-Moor Corp.

Name_____

Day 1 propose • proposal

1. How would you complete these sentences? Say them aloud to a partner.

When you propose an idea, it is important to _____.

I would like to make a proposal to my parents about _____.

2. Which word is a synonym for *propose*? Circle your answer.

a. accept   c. require

b. approve   d. suggest

3. Which sentence does not use *proposal* correctly? Circle your answer.

a. I need to do more research before I write my proposal.

b. Can you proposal a way to pay for new team uniforms?

c. Your proposal was the best idea of all.

d. The team's proposal was rejected by the coach.

4. If you were in charge of planning a class party, what would you *propose*?

_____

_____

Day 2 proposition

1. How would you complete this sentence? Say it aloud to a partner.

I think students in our school would support a proposition to _____.

2. Which of these would you not expect to find in a *proposition* to add more days to the school year? Circle your answer.

a. reasons for why more school days are needed

b. an explanation of the effect of having more school days

c. reasons for why there are already too many school days

d. suggestions for specific days to add to the school year

3. Which of these sentences are *propositions*? Circle your answers.

a. I'll do the dishes for three days if you let me go to the movie.

b. We can go to the pool on Saturday, and I'll teach you how to swim.

c. The last thing I did this morning was brush my teeth.

d. Dogs are very loving pets.

**Daily
Academic
Vocabulary**

Day 3 intend

1. How would you complete this sentence? Say it aloud to a partner.

After school today, I intend to _____.

**2. Match the person with the thing that he or she might *intend* to do.
Write the correct letter on the line.**

___ runner

___ postal worker

___ singer

___ writer

a. publish a book of stories

b. appear in a musical

c. win a big race

d. finish delivering mail by 3:30 p.m.

3. List three goals that you *intend* to meet this year in school.

a. _____

b. _____

c. _____

Day 4 intention

1. How would you complete this sentence? Say it aloud to a partner.

My intention is to be the best _____ I can be.

2. Which word is a synonym for *intention*? Circle your answer.

a. goal

b. success

c. effort

d. achievement

3. Which of these is the most accurate statement about an *intention*? Circle your answer.

a. It is something that you plan to study in school.

b. It is something that you want to do.

c. It is something that only happens in stories.

d. It is something that you would do only if you had to.

Name_____

| **Day 5** | **propose • proposal • proposition**
intend • intention |

Fill in the bubble next to the correct answer.

1. Which sentence uses both *propose* and *proposal* correctly?

Ⓐ The propose went well, but the proposal was still rejected.

Ⓑ They liked the proposal after the propose.

Ⓒ You should proposal any ideas you want to propose.

Ⓓ Any ideas you propose should be explained in a proposal.

2. Which of these is not true of a *proposition*?

Ⓕ It is a type of plan.

Ⓖ It is usually a secret.

Ⓗ It can be accepted or rejected.

Ⓙ It makes an offer to be considered.

3. To *intend* means to _____.

Ⓐ plan to do something

Ⓑ work on something

Ⓒ show something

Ⓓ imagine something

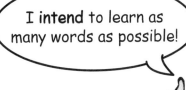

I intend to learn as many words as possible!

4. Which sentence does not use *intention* correctly?

Ⓕ Our intention is to form a group of volunteers.

Ⓖ The intention of each volunteer is to help others.

Ⓗ We intention to work with children.

Ⓙ It is our intention to raise money for the school.

Writing   *Propose* a new award for students in your school. Use the words *propose* and *proposal* in your writing.

_____

_____

_____

_____

exaggerate • exaggeration
minimize • minimum • minimal

Use the reproducible definitions on page 162 and the suggestions on page 6 to introduce the words for each day.

DAY 1

exaggerate
(verb) To make something seem larger, more valuable, or more important than it is. *Drawings sometimes **exaggerate** the size of a shark's teeth.*

exaggeration
(noun) The act of exaggerating. *It is an **exaggeration** to say that I can hit a ball clear into the next county.*

Make a statement that is an obvious **exaggeration**, such as, *I'm so hungry I could eat a horse.* Say: *I just **exaggerated**, or stretched the truth. I am hungry, but certainly not hungry enough to literally eat a horse.* Ask: *What do people do when they **exaggerate**?* Ask: *What kinds of stories do we read that have **exaggerated**, or larger-than-life, characters?* (tall tales) Write "**exaggeration**" on the board. Use a different color for "-tion." Point out that the suffix "-tion" means "the act or state of." Then say: *When you **exaggerate**, the result is an **exaggeration**.* Discuss some of the **exaggerations** students have read in tall tales. Invite students to make up **exaggerations**. Then have students complete the Day 1 activities on page 19. You may want to do the first one as a group.

DAY 2

minimize
(verb) To make something as small as possible. *We can **minimize** the amount of work for each student if we work together as a team.*

Write the prefix "mini-" on the board and discuss its meaning with students. (small) Write "**minimize**" on the board. Ask: *What are some things we might wish to **minimize**?* (e.g., amount of time wasted) Then have students complete the Day 2 activities on page 19. You may want to do the first one as a group.

DAY 3

minimum
(noun) The smallest possible amount or lowest limit. *One dollar is the **minimum** that you can donate to the fund.*

Use students' knowledge of the prefix "mini-" to help them understand **minimum**. Say: *When you minimize something, you create the **minimum**, the smallest amount or lowest limit. What is the **minimum** age for driving a car?* Then have students complete the Day 3 activities on page 20. You may want to do the first one as a group.

DAY 4

minimal
(adj.) Being the smallest in amount or size. *It takes **minimal** effort to smile, but the rewards are big.*

Explain that **minimal** is an adjective that describes something that is the smallest in amount or size. Ask questions such as: *Which would take a **minimal** amount of time, sharpening a pencil or painting a house? If you put **minimal** effort into a project, how do you think it would turn out?* Have students complete the Day 4 activities on page 20. You may want to do the first one as a group.

DAY 5

Have students complete page 21. Call on students to read aloud their answers to the writing activity.

Name_____

Daily
Academic
Vocabulary

Day 1 exaggerate • exaggeration

1. **How would you complete these sentences? Say them aloud to a partner.**

   Something that people exaggerate about is _____.

   An exaggeration might be, "My room is _____."

2. **Which phrase describes what people do when they *exaggerate*? Circle your answer.**

   a. hide the truth   c. discover the truth
   b. stretch the truth   d. tell the truth

3. **Which of these is the best example of something that shows *exaggeration* in a story? Circle your answer.**

   a. a character with superhuman strength   c. a plot with a surprise ending
   b. a familiar theme, such as friendship   d. a setting that takes place long ago

4. **Write about a time you *exaggerated*.**

   _____

   _____

Day 2 minimize

1. **How would you complete this sentence? Say it aloud to a partner.**

   I think people should minimize _____.

2. **Which sentence uses *minimize* correctly? Circle your answer.**

   a. Students can minimize the desks in their classroom.
   b. Students can minimize the lunch period by eating slowly.
   c. Students can minimize noise by speaking quietly.
   d. Students can minimize their lockers by keeping them neat.

3. **What is the result if your teacher agrees to *minimize* the amount of homework? Circle your answer.**

   a. You would get no homework.
   b. You would get more homework.
   c. You would get more time for homework.
   d. You would get less homework.

Name_____

Daily
Academic
Vocabulary

Day 3 minimum

1. How would you complete this sentence? Say it aloud to a partner.

The minimum amount of time I spend on homework is _____.

2. Which word would you associate with the meaning of *minimum*? Circle your answer.

a. best   c. less

b. least   d. worst

3. A contest requires an essay that has a *minimum* of 200 words. Which of these would eliminate you from the contest? Circle your answer.

a. writing an essay of 200 words

b. writing an essay of more than 200 words

c. writing an essay of less than 200 words

d. writing an essay with 200 words on each page

4. If your teacher asks you to keep your talking to a *minimum*, what does that mean?

_____

_____

Day 4 minimal

1. How would you complete this sentence? Say it aloud to a partner.

_____ is an activity that used to be hard for me, but now it takes minimal effort.

2. If a storm did *minimal* damage, which adjective would be best for describing the storm? Circle your answer.

a. huge   c. major

b. terrible   d. mild

3. Which of these would require *minimal* care? Circle your answer.

a. a cactus   c. a baby

b. a dog   d. a horse

Name _____

Daily
Academic
Vocabulary

Fill in the bubble next to the correct answer.

1. Which statement is correct?

I caught a fish that was as big as a whale!

Ⓐ An exaggeration is a made-up character.

Ⓑ To exaggerate means to tell a secret.

Ⓒ You cannot exaggerate when you talk.

Ⓓ An exaggeration can make something seem bigger than it is.

2. Which word is the opposite of *minimize*?

Ⓕ increase

Ⓖ improve

Ⓗ decrease

Ⓘ big

3. If you do the *minimum* on an assignment, which of these describes your behavior?

Ⓐ You do more than you need to do.

Ⓑ You do less than you need to do.

Ⓒ You do only what you are required to do.

Ⓓ You do only what you want to do.

4. Which adjective means the same as *minimal*?

Ⓕ slow

Ⓖ smallest

Ⓗ massive

Ⓘ small

Writing   Write an *exaggeration* about a time you were hungry.

_____

_____

_____

_____

unique • identical dissimilar • equivalent

Use the reproducible definitions on page 163 and the suggestions on page 6 to introduce the words for each day.

DAY 1

unique
(adj.) Being the only one of its kind. *The painting is* **unique** *because it is the only one by this artist.*

Explain that **unique** is an adjective that describes something that is one of a kind, and not just special or rare. Say: *You use the word* **unique** *by itself. We do not say "most* **unique***" or "really* **unique***" because* **unique** *is one of a kind.* Give students the example of fingerprints. Say: *Scientists say no two people have the same fingerprints. That means that the pattern of swirls on your fingers is* **unique**. *What other things are* **unique**? Then have students complete the Day 1 activities on page 23. You may want to do the first one as a group.

DAY 2

identical
(adj.) Exactly alike. *No two days in school are* **identical** *because something different happens each day.*

Have on hand three objects, two of which are exactly alike. (e.g., two pieces of unused chalk and a third that is of a different length) Say: **Identical** *objects are exactly alike in every way.* Hold up the pieces of chalk for students to compare. Ask: *Which pieces are* **identical**? *Why is the third piece* not **identical**, *even though it is also a piece of chalk?* Then have students complete the Day 2 activities on page 23. You may want to do the first one as a group.

DAY 3

dissimilar
(adj.) Not alike; different. *Even though they are twins, the girls are* **dissimilar**.

Ask: *If the prefix "dis-" means "not," what does* **dissimilar** *mean?* Ask: *What are two things in this classroom that are* **dissimilar**? *What makes them* **dissimilar**? Have several students respond. Encourage them to use the word **dissimilar** in their responses. Then have students complete the Day 3 activities on page 24. You may want to do the first one as a group.

DAY 4

equivalent
(adj.) The same as, or equal to, another thing. *The winter break from school is shorter than summer vacation. They are not* **equivalent**.

Write **equivalent** on the board. Underline the prefix "equi-" and explain that it means "equal." Explain that **equivalent** means "the same as" or "equal to" something else. Hold up a dime. Then hold up two nickels. Ask: *Are these things* **equivalent**? *Why or why not?* Repeat with other examples of items or ideas that are and are not **equivalent**. Then have students complete the Day 4 activities on page 24. You may want to do the first one as a group.

DAY 5

Have students complete page 25. Call on students to read aloud their answers to the writing activity.

Name_____

Day 1 unique

1. **How would you complete this sentence? Say it aloud to a partner.**

   Something that makes me unique is _____.

2. **Which word is an antonym for *unique*? Circle your answer.**

   a. different   c. unusual

   b. common   d. ugly

3. **The teacher says that your topic for the science report is *unique.*
   What does that mean? Circle your answer.**

   a. Several other students have chosen the same topic.

   b. Your topic has been done many times in the past.

   c. You have the best idea for a topic in the class.

   d. You are the only student who thought of that topic.

4. **What is something you have that is *unique*?**

   _____

   _____

Day 2 identical

1. **How would you complete this sentence? Say it aloud to a partner.**

   A friend who had identical interests to mine would like _____.

2. **Which sentence uses *identical* correctly? Circle your answer.**

   a. The elephant and giraffe at the zoo were identical.

   b. The lockers are identical, with different colors and sizes.

   c. Our reading books are identical, so everyone has the same stories.

   d. Many sports are identical because they all use a ball.

3. **Which word is a synonym for *identical*? Circle your answer.**

   a. matching   c. interesting

   b. similar   d. special

Day 3 dissimilar

1. How would you complete this sentence? Say it aloud to a partner.

Two dissimilar interests I have are _____ and _____.

2. If two books are *dissimilar,* which statement is probably true about them? Circle your answer.

a. They are written by the same author and have the same characters.
b. They are the same book, but one is an older copy.
c. They are on different topics and written by different authors.
d. They are on the same topic and have the same number of pages.

3. Which word would <u>not</u> describe two people who are *dissimilar?* Circle your answer.

a. same   c. different
b. opposite   d. unlike

4. Can two people who are *dissimilar* still be friends? Why or why not?

_____

_____

Day 4 equivalent

1. How would you complete this sentence? Say it aloud to a partner.

There is no school that is equivalent to ours because _____.

2. A writing partner suggests you change a word to one with an *equivalent* meaning. What kind of word do you need? Circle your answer.

a. a word with a different meaning   c. a word that has many meanings
b. a word that is easier to understand   d. a word with the same meaning

3. If two foods are *equivalent* in calories, which statement is true about them? Circle your answer.

a. One food is better for you than the other.
b. Both foods have an equal number of calories.
c. Both foods look and taste exactly alike.
d. Both foods are high in calories.

Name_____

Day 5 | unique • identical • dissimilar • equivalent

Fill in the bubble next to the correct answer.

1. A *unique* gift is _____.

Ⓐ one of a kind

Ⓑ attractive

Ⓒ easy to find

Ⓓ breakable

2. If two sounds are *identical,* they are _____.

Ⓕ quiet

Ⓖ loud

Ⓗ alike

Ⓙ distinctive

3. Two *dissimilar* sports _____.

Ⓐ use the same equipment

Ⓑ have the same rules

Ⓒ are unpopular

Ⓓ are different in many ways

4. If two sums are *equivalent,* they _____.

Ⓕ are both big numbers

Ⓖ are equal in value

Ⓗ are difficult to add

Ⓙ can be divided by 12

You must admit that I am truly **unique**.

Writing   What makes each person a *unique* individual? Explain your ideas.
Use the word *unique* in your writing.

_____

_____

_____

_____

narrate • narrator
narrative • narration

Use the reproducible definitions on page 164 and the suggestions on page 6 to introduce the words for each day.

DAY 1

narrate
(verb) To tell the story or give an account of something in speech or writing. *Each team member will **narrate** a portion of the presentation.*

Say: ***Narrate** means that someone tells the story or gives information, often while other action goes on. Stories, movies, poems, books, and plays can all be **narrated**.* Ask: *Where or when have you heard someone **narrate** something?* (e.g., readers' theater; books; movies) *Have you ever **narrated** something? What was it?* Then have students complete the Day 1 activities on page 27. You may want to do the first one as a group.

DAY 2

narrator
(noun) A person or character who tells a story. *The play has a **narrator** who introduces all the characters.*

Say: *The person who narrates something is called the **narrator**.* Ask: *What are some examples of stories, movies, poems, books, or plays with a **narrator**?* (e.g., *March of the Penguins; Casey at the Bat; Alice in Wonderland*) Then have students complete the Day 2 activities on page 27. You may want to do the first one as a group.

DAY 3

narrative
(noun) A story, description, or account of events. *The assignment was to write a **narrative** about your first day of school.*

Say: *In school, you may hear the term "personal **narrative**." Based on the definition of **narrative**, what do you think that term means?* (an account of an event in your own life) To test students' understanding of **narrative**, ask: *What is an example of a personal **narrative** you have had to write for school?* (e.g., description of summer vacation) Then ask: *What is an example of a writing assignment that is <u>not a</u> **narrative**?* (e.g., book reports; social studies reports) Then have students complete the Day 3 activities on page 28. You may want to do the first one as a group.

DAY 4

narration
(noun) The act of narrating. *The concert will include music and **narration** about the history of our country.*

Say: *A narrator does the **narration** for something.* Ask two dramatic students to stand in front of the class. Tell one student to silently enact swimming in a race. Have the other student narrate the action. Ask the class: *Who was the narrator? What did he (or she) narrate? What did you think of his (or her) **narration**?* Encourage students to use the vocabulary words in their responses. Then have students complete the Day 4 activities on page 28. You may want to do the first one as a group.

DAY 5

Have students complete page 29. Call on students to read aloud their answers to the writing activity.

Name_____

Day 1 narrate

1. How would you complete this sentence? Say it aloud to a partner.

In order to narrate a story, I would need to _____.

2. A test question asks you to *narrate* an account of a memorable birthday. Which statement describes what you need to do? Circle your answer.

    a. Write a description of what happened on a special birthday.

    b. Analyze a reading passage about a special birthday.

    c. Find the total cost of a special birthday party.

    d. Think of a title for a story about what happened on a special birthday.

3. Which of these might you do if you were asked to *narrate* a presentation of a folk tale? Circle your answer.

    a. be a character in the folk tale

    b. introduce the characters of the story and describe the things they do

    c. wait to see the movie based on the story

    d. write another story

4. What is a story, play, or movie you would like to *narrate*?

_____

Day 2 narrator

1. How would you complete this sentence? Say it aloud to a partner.

To do a good job as a narrator, you need to _____.

2. Which of these explains what the *narrator* of a movie does? Circle your answer.

    a. makes the costumes for the characters in the movie

    b. doesn't say anything

    c. watches the movie

    d. tells the audience important story details

3. Which type of story always has a *narrator*? Circle your answer.

    a. an article that describes an important historical event

    b. a story in which one character describes the action

    c. a science fiction tale

    d. a fairy tale

Day 3 narrative

1. How would you complete this sentence? Say it aloud to a partner.

A narrative about my typical school day would include _____.

2. You have an assignment to write a *narrative* about something you did with a friend. Which of the following would fit the assignment? Circle your answer.

    a. a list of Web sites about friends

    b. a report on what your friend looks like

    c. a card that you would send to the friend

    d. an account of the time you both camped out in the backyard

3. Which sentence uses *narrative* correctly? Circle your answer.

    a. Each student will have a chance to narrative a story.

    b. The narrative did not speak loud enough for everyone to hear.

    c. Her narrative about her week at camp was as exciting as an adventure story.

    d. The movie was hard to understand and needed a character to narrative.

Day 4 narration

1. How would you complete this sentence? Say it aloud to a partner.

Something that I recently saw or heard that had narration was _____.

2. Your teacher asks the class to write a *narration* for photographs of the class field trip to present to parents. What is the class doing? Circle your answer.

    a. writing descriptions of the photographs to be read aloud

    b. writing the names of everyone in the photographs

    c. writing thank-you letters to the bus driver and tour guide

    d. writing a list of facts students learned on the field trip

3. Which sentence uses *narration* correctly? Circle your answer.

    a. You need a good voice to be a narration.

    b. The play had a character who was the narration.

    c. Many famous actors narration audiobooks.

    d. The movie began with a narration that introduced the characters.

4. How would you prepare if you were to do a *narration* of a book?

_____

_____

Name_____

Day 5 narrate • narrator • narrative • narration

Fill in the bubble next to the correct answer.

1. Which of these would you most likely be asked to *narrate*?

Ⓐ the title of a book

Ⓑ a list of things you had for lunch yesterday

Ⓒ your home telephone number

Ⓓ a story about something that happened to you

2. Which word is a synonym for *narrator*?

Ⓕ librarian

Ⓖ storyteller

Ⓗ artist

Ⓙ leader

3. Which word is <u>not</u> a synonym for *narrative*?

Ⓐ account

Ⓑ tale

Ⓒ newspaper

Ⓓ description

4. Which word explains the purpose of *narration*?

Ⓕ telling

Ⓖ seeing

Ⓗ guessing

Ⓙ hiding

Once upon a time, there was a handsome parrot...

Writing   Explain some of the things you would include in a *narrative* about your favorite field trip. Be sure to include the word *narrative* in your writing.

_____

_____

_____

_____

Daily Academic Vocabulary

demonstrate • demonstration establish

Use the reproducible definitions on page 165 and the suggestions on page 6 to introduce the words for each day.

DAY 1

demonstrate
(verb) To teach or explain by showing how to do or use something. *The coach will demonstrate the proper way to hold a bat.*

demonstration
(noun) An act of teaching, explaining, or operating something. *The health class will get a demonstration of how to clean a cut.*

Say: *This common meaning of demonstrate involves showing how to do or use things.* Ask a student to **demonstrate** how to multiply two-digit numbers. After the demonstration, say: *(Student's name) demonstrated how to multiply two-digit numbers. He (or she) gave us a demonstration. He (or she) taught and explained how to multiply two-digit numbers.* Ask: *In what school situations are demonstrations usually given?* Encourage students to use the words **demonstrate** and **demonstration** in their responses. Then have students complete the Day 1 activities on page 31. You may want to do the first one as a group.

DAY 2

demonstrate
(verb) To prove or show clearly. *A capable lawyer will demonstrate her client's innocence.*

Say: *This definition of demonstrate involves proving something, as opposed to teaching or showing how to do something. For example, we would say that research has demonstrated that eating junk food is bad for you. That sentence shows that something has been proven.* Ask: *What else has research demonstrated?* (e.g., smoking is bad for you; the number of moons around Saturn) Then have students complete the Day 2 activities on page 31. You may want to do the first one as a group.

DAY 3

establish
(verb) To prove or show something to be true. *The attendance count will establish that most students in our school are present today.*

Say: *Establish can mean to prove or show something to be true.* Ask: *What can we establish about our class? What can we prove or show about it that is true?* (e.g., number of students) Make sure that students use the correct definition of **establish**. Then have students complete the Day 3 activities on page 32. You may want to do the first one as a group.

DAY 4

establish
(verb) To create or start. *The school will establish a new award to recognize good conduct.*

Say: *This year we have established, or created, our classroom rules.* Ask: *What are some examples of things you would like to see established, either created or started, in your community?* (e.g., new businesses; parks; activities for kids) Then have students complete the Day 4 activities on page 32. You may want to do the first one as a group.

DAY 5

Have students complete page 33. Call on students to read aloud their answers to the writing activity.

Day 1 · demonstrate • demonstration

1. How would you complete these sentences? Say them aloud to a partner.

I can demonstrate how to _____.

I have seen a demonstration of _____.

2. Which of these are required to *demonstrate* how to paint with watercolors? Circle your answer.

- a. a pencil and crayons
- b. visits to an art museum
- c. books about artists
- d. a paintbrush and watercolors

3. Which of these would be a *demonstration* of what to do in a fire drill? Circle your answer.

- a. A student refuses to get up from his desk.
- b. A student writes a report on fire drills.
- c. A student gets up from his desk and leaves the classroom in an orderly way.
- d. A student shows the class that fire is dangerous.

4. What would you like to see a *demonstration* of?

_____

Day 2 · demonstrate

1. How would you complete this sentence? Say it aloud to a partner.

I can demonstrate that something floats by _____.

2. Which of these would <u>not</u> help you *demonstrate* that you are a responsible student? Circle your answer.

- a. turning in homework on time
- b. saying that you will be responsible from now on
- c. obeying school rules
- d. completing your share of a team project

3. Which of these would *demonstrate* that a team needs new uniforms? Circle your answer.

- a. lots of rips and tears in the old uniforms
- b. players who do not like the old uniforms
- c. pictures of new uniforms
- d. pictures of another team with new uniforms

These *glasses* **demonstrate** that I am one cool bird!

Day 3 | establish

1. How would you complete this sentence? Say it aloud to a partner.

I can establish that I am _____ by _____.

2. You are reading about how a scientist worked to *establish* a theory. What are you learning? Circle your answer.

   a. why the scientist refused to believe the theory

   b. how to write a science report

   c. how the scientist built her lab

   d. how the scientist proved the theory was correct

3. Which of these would best help you *establish* that you have musical talent? Circle your answer.

   a. singing a song in the school concert

   b. knowing the names of all the musical instruments in a band

   c. listening to music every day

   d. talking about music with your friends

Day 4 | establish

1. How would you complete this sentence? Say it aloud to a partner.

One thing I can do to establish good study habits is _____.

2. A history test asks a question about efforts to *establish* the United States as a country. Which of the following is most likely to be the question? Circle your answer.

   a. How did the United States come into being?

   b. What is the present size and population of the United States?

   c. How can you prove that the United States is a country?

   d. What will the United States be like in 50 years?

3. Which of these would you <u>not</u> need in order to *establish* a new sports team at school? Circle your answer.

   a. students who want to be on the team   c. equipment to play the sport

   b. trophies for outstanding players   d. a coach for the team

4. What club, team, or activity would you like to *establish* at your school?

_____

Name_____

Daily Academic Vocabulary

Day 5 demonstrate • demonstration • establish

Fill in the bubble next to the correct answer.

1. Which pair of words are both synonyms for *demonstrate*?

Ⓐ see—hear

Ⓑ prove—instruct

Ⓒ hide—tell

Ⓓ agree—refuse

2. In which sentence could *demonstration* be used to fill in the blank?

Ⓕ A chef will _____ to show others how to cook.

Ⓖ For our science project we can _____ how a battery works.

Ⓗ The swimming coach is a good _____ for how to dive.

Ⓘ A _____ will help us understand how to use the camera.

3. Which of these would *establish* that a school rule was broken?

Ⓐ a list of school rules

Ⓑ students who disagree with the rule

Ⓒ proof that the rule was broken

Ⓓ a student in the principal's office

4. To *establish* a rock-collecting club, you would need _____.

Ⓕ friends who also enjoyed collecting rocks and wanted to join

Ⓖ a lot of rocks in your backyard

Ⓗ to show that there already was such a club

Ⓘ to go shopping

Writing How can you *demonstrate* that you are a good friend to others?
Use one of this week's words in your writing.

_____

_____

_____

_____

WEEK 7

trait • characteristic • character characterize • property

Use the reproducible definitions on page 166 and the suggestions on page 6 to introduce the words for each day.

DAY 1

trait
(noun) A special quality or feature of a person or animal. *Creativity is a **trait** that most artists have.*

Say: ***Traits** often describe the appearance, behavior, or personality of people or animals.* Ask: *What are **traits**, or qualities, that you want in a friend?* (e.g., honest; kind; funny) *What are **traits** you want in a teacher?* (e.g., patient; smart) Then have students complete the Day 1 activities on page 35. You may want to do the first one as a group.

DAY 2

characteristic
(noun) A regular quality or feature of someone or something. *Fast action is a **characteristic** of a soccer game.*

character
(noun) All of the many things that make one person or thing different from another. *The parks and playgrounds in this neighborhood give it a friendly **character**.*

Explain that **characteristics** are like *traits,* but they are more general qualities that you associate with a type of person or thing. For example, ask: *What are qualities of a firefighter?* (e.g., courageous; quick-thinking) Say: *Not every firefighter has these qualities, but these are general **characteristics** we associate with firefighters.* Then point out the word **character** in **characteristic.** Students will know that a **character** is a person in a story. Say: ***Character** also means the total of the **characteristics** of a person or thing. For example, Abraham Lincoln's **character** can be described as honest and fair.* Have students think of other famous people and describe their **character.** Then have students complete the Day 2 activities on page 35. You may want to do the first one as a group.

DAY 3

characterize
(verb) To describe the character and qualities of someone or something. *You could **characterize** life in a city as noisy and busy.*

Tell students about a movie you have seen. Say: *I would **characterize** the movie as (funny; sad; scary).* Then invite students to tell about a movie they've seen. Ask: *How would you **characterize** it? What are its characteristics?* Then have students complete the Day 3 activities on page 36. You may want to do the first one as a group.

DAY 4

property
(noun) A distinctive physical characteristic of something; a common quality of all things belonging to a particular group. *One **property** of oxygen is that is has no smell.*

Say: ***Properties** are physical characteristics. They are always true and do not change.* Hold up a bottle of glue and say: *What are the **properties** of glue? What is always true?* Point out that glue is not always runny. When it dries, it becomes hard. However, glue always makes things stick together. Stickiness is a **property** of glue. Then have students complete the Day 4 activities on page 36. You may want to do the first one as a group.

DAY 5

Have students complete page 37. Call on students to read aloud their answers to the writing activity.

Name_____

Day 1   trait

1. How would you complete this sentence? Say it aloud to a partner.

One of my personality traits is _____.

2. Think of a character in a book you have read. What *traits* does the character have?

a. _____

b. _____

c. _____

One of my most noticeable **traits** is my good looks.

3. Which word is a synonym for *trait?* Circle your answer.

a. personality
b. description
c. quality
d. sign

Day 2   characteristic • character

1. How would you complete these sentences? Say them aloud to a partner.

An elephant's characteristics are _____.

A principal's character is often _____.

2. Which sentence does _not_ use *characteristic* correctly? Circle your answer.

a. Curly hair is a characteristic of some families.
b. Stripes are a characteristic of the zebra.
c. One characteristic of poetry is rhyme.
d. The person in the book was characteristic.

3. Think about your own *character.* What are three *characteristics* you can name?

a. _____

b. _____

c. _____

Daily
Academic
Vocabulary

Day 3 characterize

1. **How would you complete this sentence? Say it aloud to a partner.**

   I would characterize my school as _____.

2. **Which of these *characterizes* a poorly written paragraph? Circle your answers.**

   a. exciting language   c. no main idea

   b. many errors   d. funny

3. **What *characterizes* a good song? List three characteristics.**

   a. _____

   b. _____

   c. _____

4. **How would you *characterize* the last book you read? Complete the chart.**

Good Characteristics	Bad Characteristics

Day 4 property

1. **How would you complete this sentence? Say it aloud to a partner.**

   Some of the properties of modeling clay are _____.

2. **Which of these things are *properties* of sugar? Circle your answers.**

   a. forms as crystals   c. tastes bitter

   b. dissolves in liquid   d. wet

3. **Which word is a synonym for the word *property*? Circle your answer.**

   a. characteristic   c. chemical

   b. condition   d. difference

Day 5 · trait • characteristic • character
characterize • property

Fill in the bubble next to the correct answer.

1. Which sentence uses the word *trait* correctly?

Ⓐ A common trait of cats is curiosity.

Ⓑ A good friend has the trait of a nice home.

Ⓒ One trait of nurses is that they go to college.

Ⓓ The rock has the trait of being shiny.

2. Which of the following is <u>not</u> a common *characteristic* of a typical scientist?

Ⓕ intelligent

Ⓖ curious

Ⓗ careless

Ⓙ careful

3. Which sentence does <u>not</u> use the word *character* correctly?

Ⓐ A mother should have a kind and patient character.

Ⓑ One character of a guide dog is that it obeys its master.

Ⓒ The movie star's rude, unfriendly character won him no friends.

Ⓓ The room had a warm, inviting character.

4. Which sentence describes a *property*?

Ⓕ A property is an animal trait.

Ⓖ A property describes the character of something.

Ⓗ A property is always true and does not change.

Ⓙ A property describes a person's personality.

Writing   How would you *characterize* the city or town where you live?
Use at least one of this week's words in your writing.

_____

_____

_____

_____

WEEK 8

option • optional
essential • vital

Use the reproducible definitions on page 167 and the suggestions on page 6 to introduce the words for each day.

DAY 1

option
(noun) One of several things that can be chosen. *Pizza is one option for lunch today.*

Say: *An option is what is available or what can be chosen.* Ask: *What options do you have for after-school activities?* (e.g., sports; clubs) *Have you ever heard the phrase "consider your options?" What do you think that means?* Then have students complete the Day 1 activities on page 39. You may want to do the first one as a group.

DAY 2

optional
(adj.) Left to your own choice to do; not required. *Attending school is not optional for most students.*

Say: *Sometimes we are not required to do certain things. We can make the choice whether to do them or not. We say that those things are optional.* Ask: *Which activities in school are optional?* (e.g., joining school clubs and teams) *Why are they optional?* (e.g., not necessary for academic success) Then ask: *If you are filling out a form and see a section labeled optional, what does that mean?* (don't have to complete it) Then have students complete the Day 2 activities on page 39. You may want to do the first one as a group.

DAY 3

essential
(adj.) Very important or necessary. *Learning to read is an essential skill.*

(noun) A necessary thing to have. *One essential for learning to read is a book.*

Say: *The word essential can be used as either an adjective or a noun, but the meanings are related. For example, breathing is essential. It is necessary to live. Breathing is one of the essentials for life.* Ask: *What is the difference between essential and "optional"?* Then ask students to name other actions they think are essential. (e.g., eating; sleeping) Ask them to name essentials needed for life. (e.g., food; water) Encourage students to use the word essential in their responses. Then have students complete the Day 3 activities on page 40. You may want to do the first one as a group.

DAY 4

vital
(adj.) Very important or essential. *Getting enough calcium is vital for strong bones.*

Ask: *What other word have we learned this week that is a synonym for vital?* (essential) Ask: *What things are vital for good health?* (e.g., good food; exercise) *What things are vital to an animal?* (e.g., food; water; shelter) *What things are vital to your life?* Encourage students to use the word vital in their responses. Then have students complete the Day 4 activities on page 40. You may want to do the first one as a group.

DAY 5

Have students complete page 41. Call on students to read aloud their answers to the writing activity.

Day 1 option

1. How would you complete this sentence? Say it aloud to a partner.

One option I always have for an after-school activity is _____.

2. Which word is a synonym for *option*? Circle your answer.

a. selection   c. requirement

b. choice   d. belief

3. What are your *options* of things to do this weekend? List three of them.

a. _____

b. _____

c. _____

Day 2 optional

1. How would you complete this sentence? Say it aloud to a partner.

One school subject that I feel should be optional is _____.

2. The teacher announces that today's quiz is *optional*. What does that mean? Circle your answer.

a. Everyone in the class must take the quiz.

b. Only some students in the class must take the quiz.

c. The teacher changed her mind about giving the quiz.

d. Each student can choose whether to take the quiz.

3. Which sentence uses *optional* correctly? Circle your answer.

a. Optional activities at camp are fishing and bird-watching.

b. We have one optional for a movie to watch tonight.

c. The optional question must be answered to complete the test.

d. The show was so optional that I couldn't stop laughing.

4. Which activities or subjects are *optional* at your school?

_____

Name_____

Day 3 essential

1. How would you complete these sentences? Say them aloud to a partner.

One of the essential things I do before school is _____.

Something that many kids consider an essential is a(n) _____.

2. Which adjective is a synonym for *essential*? Circle your answer.

   a. flexible   c. exciting

   b. critical   d. extra

3. Which objects are *essentials* in a classroom? Circle your answer.

   a. posters   c. books

   b. plants   d. aquariums

4. What activity is *essential* to you?

_____

Nuts are a dietary **essential**!

Day 4 vital

1. How would you complete this sentence? Say it aloud to a partner.

To be good at a sport, it is vital to _____.

2. Your teacher says the class will discuss *vital* events that are happening in the world today. What does that mean? Circle your answer.

   a. The class will discuss every event in the history of the world.

   b. The class will discuss the most important current world events.

   c. The class discussion is an important event.

   d. There are discussions happening in the world today.

3. Which word is an antonym for *vital*? Circle your answer.

   a. essential   c. unnecessary

   b. unusual   d. unhappy

4. What resources are *vital* for plant life?

_____

Name_____

Day 5 option • optional • essential • vital

Fill in the bubble next to the correct answer.

1. Which list gives several different *options* for ways to get home from school?

Ⓐ a bus, a steering wheel, a seat

Ⓑ a door, a window, the sidewalk

Ⓒ a bus, a bicycle, walking

Ⓓ a plane, an elevator, a shopping cart

2. In which sentence could *optional* replace the underlined word?

Ⓕ Practice today is <u>required</u> for all team members.

Ⓖ New uniforms are <u>needed</u> this year.

Ⓗ The coaches have <u>busy</u> schedules this year.

Ⓙ Attending the team dinner is <u>voluntary</u> this year.

3. Which sentence uses *essential* correctly?

Ⓐ A passport is essential to visit another country.

Ⓑ A stove is the essential that we don't need to have.

Ⓒ We can essential food for a few days.

Ⓓ I like to travel with my essential.

4. In which sentence could the word *vital* fill in the blank?

Ⓕ The recipe will taste as good without that _____ ingredient.

Ⓖ If that step is _____, we can skip it.

Ⓗ Reading to the end is _____ for understanding the story.

Ⓙ The plan was _____ and soon forgotten.

Writing   What qualities or behaviors are *essential* for success in school? Include the word *essential* in your writing.

_____

_____

_____

_____

_____

CUMULATIVE REVIEW
WORDS FROM WEEKS 1–8

character
characteristic
characterize
conceive
concept
conceptualize
demonstrate
demonstration
dissimilar
equivalent
essential
establish
exaggerate
exaggeration
identical
inconceivable
intend
intention
minimal
minimize
minimum
narrate
narration
narrative
narrator
option
optional
property
proposal
propose
proposition
trait
unique
vital

Days 1–4

Each day's activity is a cloze paragraph that students complete with words or forms of words that they have learned in weeks 1–8. Before students begin, pronounce each word in the box on the student page, have students repeat each word, and then review each word's meaning(s). **Other ways to review the words:**

- Start a sentence containing one of the words and have students finish the sentence orally. For example:

  The **essential** rules for a school are...
  I could **conceive** a plan to...

- Provide students with a definition and ask them to supply the word that fits it.

- Ask questions that require students to know the meaning of each word. For example:

  What makes you **unique**?
  What are the **traits** of a good book?

- Have students use each word in a sentence.

Day 5

Start by reviewing the words in the crossword puzzle activity for Day 5. Write the words on the board and have students repeat them after you. Provide a sentence for one of the words. Ask students to think of their own sentence and share it with a partner. Call on several students to share their sentences. Follow the same procedure for the remaining words. Then have students complete the crossword activity.

Extension Ideas

Use any of the following activities to help integrate the vocabulary words into other content areas:

- Have students write a story with a **narrator**. Students can exchange stories with each other, suggest revisions, and then revise their own stories.

- Have students write a **proposal** for a class field trip.

- Have students use a graphic organizer to **demonstrate** how plants convert sunlight into energy.

- Have students give a **demonstration** on the **properties** of the three states of water. (liquid, ice, vapor)

- Have students **conceive** a way to teach younger students about the **essential** people in a certain period of history.

Daily Academic Vocabulary

| characteristic | dissimilar | establish | intended | narrative |
| characterized | essentials | inconceivable | minimal | vital |

Day 1

Fill in the blanks with words from the word box.

Can you imagine a place that receives less than one millimeter of rain a year?

Such a place seems _____ because water is so necessary

for life. Two-thirds of a human body consists of this _____

resource. But in the Atacama Desert in Chile, it rarely rains. The lack of water is the

_____ that makes it the driest place on Earth. Rainfall is so

_____ that in some parts of the desert there is no life. In fact,

scientists have used the Atacama to _____ the smallest amount

of water any life needs to exist.

Day 2

Fill in the blanks with words from the word box.

In class, we read a _____ by a girl named Zlata Filipovic.

She kept a diary from 1991 to 1993 about her life in the Bosnian capital city of

Sarajevo. Different groups of people with _____ beliefs were

struggling to take control of the city at the time. Zlata described living in a war zone

and _____ life as difficult and scary. Survival was challenged on

a daily basis. People went for days without _____ such as food,

water, and gas. Zlata's story is amazing. If my teacher _____

for us to appreciate our lives more after reading this, it worked!

Name _____

concept	equivalent	intention	options	proposed	unique
demonstration	identical	minimum	property	proposition	

Day 3

Fill in the blanks with words from the word box.

The principal's _____ gave class credit for community service.

Several _____ would be available, including restoring a wetland

area to its natural state and visiting the elderly in retirement homes. Students would have

to spend a certain number of hours doing service to meet the _____

requirements. The _____, or purpose, of the community service was

for the students to "learn by doing." Depending on the type of service, students would

earn the _____ of one test score in the related subject.

Day 4

Fill in the blanks with words from the word box.

When it snowed, my teacher had a great idea. He _____ we

go outside to observe the characteristics of snowflakes. One _____

of snowflakes is that no two are _____, or the same. Although

most snowflakes are hexagons, each one is _____. My teacher

also taught us the idea of symmetry. This _____ means that if

you split a snowflake down the middle, each half would look the same. He conducted

a _____ in which he caught several snowflakes on a black piece

of paper. We observed the symmetry and originality of each snowflake. It was so

interesting!

Name_____

Day 5

Crossword Challenge

For each clue, write one of the words from the word box to complete the puzzle.

| character |
| conceive |
| conceptualize |
| demonstrate |
| exaggerate |
| exaggeration |
| minimize |
| narrate |
| narration |
| narrator |
| optional |
| proposal |
| trait |

Across

1. to make something seem more important than it is
4. a suggestion or plan
9. the act of narrating
11. a special quality or feature of someone
12. to make something as small as possible

Down

1. the act of exaggerating
2. not required
3. to form a concept or idea
5. to teach by showing how to do something
6. things that make one person different from another
7. to form in the mind
8. to tell the story
10. a person who tells a story

infer • inference
surmise • contemplate

Use the reproducible definitions on page 168 and the suggestions on page 6 to introduce the words for each day.

DAY 1

infer
(verb) To draw a conclusion after considering specific evidence or facts. *Students can infer from the materials on their desks that they are doing an experiment today.*

Show props such as a book, paper, and pencil. Ask: *If you saw these materials on your desk, what could you infer from them?* (e.g., today's lesson involves reading and writing) *Why did you guess that answer?* Then say: *You based your conclusion on specific things you could see—the materials—and what you know about their uses.* Discuss the process of **inferring**—using what you see (the materials) and what you know (how materials are used) to predict a likely conclusion. Then have students complete the Day 1 activities on page 47. You may want to do the first one as a group.

DAY 2

inference
(noun) A conclusion drawn by reasoning from facts and evidence. *When Sean didn't attend the audition, we made the inference that he didn't want to be in the play.*

Say: *An inference is what you make when you infer.* Ask: *What led to your inference yesterday?* (e.g., seeing the materials and knowing what they are used for) Then ask: *Can you think back and identify any inferences you have made in school recently?* Make sure students use the word **inference** in their responses. Then have students complete the Day 2 activities on page 47. You may want to do the first one as a group.

DAY 3

surmise
(verb) To draw a conclusion without certain knowledge; suppose. *I surmise that we will go on vacation this year, but my parents haven't said anything yet.*

Say: *When you surmise, you don't have the specific evidence or facts as when you infer.* Ask: *What can you surmise that we will do in class next week?* Encourage students to use the word **surmise**. Then say: *You can surmise those things because you have some clues, but you don't know exactly what we will do.* Have students complete the Day 3 activities on page 48. You may want to do the first one as a group.

DAY 4

contemplate
(verb) To think about deeply and seriously. *The teacher will contemplate the students' suggestions.*

Say: *Contemplate is often used when you are going to think seriously about something for a period of time. What kinds of things do people contemplate? In what situations would you use the word contemplate, as opposed to simply "think"?* Then have students complete the Day 4 activities on page 48. You may want to do the first one as a group.

DAY 5

Have students complete page 49. Call on students to read aloud their answers to the writing activity.

Name_____

Day 1 infer

1. How would you complete this sentence? Say it aloud to a partner.

You can infer how popular a celebrity is by _____.

2. Which word is a synonym for *infer*? Circle your answer.

   a. choose   c. determine

   b. interrupt   d. concentrate

3. Which sentence uses *infer* correctly? Circle your answer.

   a. You can infer a character's thoughts from the character's actions.

   b. To infer a character's actions, you need a magnifying glass.

   c. There are too many characters to make an infer.

   d. I could infer what he said to me several times.

4. How might you *infer* that someone had looked through your desk?

_____

_____

Day 2 inference

1. How would you complete this sentence? Say it aloud to a partner.

If a classmate is not in his or her chair, you could make the inference that _____.

2. Which of these would help you make an *inference* from a class science experiment? Circle your answer.

   a. listening to other science students, even when their facts are wrong

   b. reading your notes of what happened during the experiment

   c. watching a science fiction movie that shows an experiment

   d. taking a guess before the experiment begins

3. Which words are <u>not</u> synonyms for *inference*? Circle your answers.

   a. conclusion   c. boredom

   b. judgment   d. correction

4. What is an *inference* you can make about studying academic vocabulary?

_____

Day 3 surmise

1. How would you complete this sentence? Say it aloud to a partner.

I surmise that I will study _____ in _____ next year.

2. In which situations would it <u>not</u> be a good idea to *surmise*? Circle your answer.

   a. wondering what is for dinner

   b. thinking about the next episode of a favorite TV show

   c. choosing the correct answer to a math problem

   d. taking money to the store to buy a specific book

3. Which sentence uses *surmise* correctly? Circle your answer.

   a. The students surmise what the teacher told them.

   b. I surmise that we will play soccer, since the soccer balls are out.

   c. My birthday party was a great surmise.

   d. I surmise that our next test will be difficult.

I **surmise** that I'll win the beauty contest!

Day 4 contemplate

1. How would you complete this sentence? Say it aloud to a partner.

One important decision I contemplated was _____.

2. Which of these would you *contemplate*? Circle your answer.

   a. how to help a friend

   b. what to wear to school

   c. what to eat for lunch

   d. how to ride a bicycle

3. Which sentence does <u>not</u> use *contemplate* correctly? Circle your answer.

   a. Veejay will contemplate long and hard before deciding on a science fair project.

   b. Let's contemplate at the playground before the game.

   c. The main character in the story had to contemplate before choosing a course of action.

   d. Please consider all the options when you contemplate your decision.

4. What do you think your friends *contemplate*?

_____

Daily
Academic
Vocabulary

Day 5 **infer • inference • surmise • contemplate**

Fill in the bubble next to the correct answer.

1. Which statement is correct?

   Ⓐ When you infer, you use your imagination to create ideas.

   Ⓑ The best way to infer is to make a guess.

   Ⓒ Good observation skills can help you infer something.

   Ⓓ Knowing facts does not help you to infer.

2. In which sentence could *inference* be used to fill in the blank?

   Ⓕ An _____ is a sentence that ends in a question mark.

   Ⓖ You can make an _____ about the subject of a book from its title.

   Ⓗ You can _____ to get an idea of how much something will cost.

   Ⓙ An _____ is a picture or drawing.

3. If you *surmise* something, which of the following explains what you do?

   Ⓐ think about it

   Ⓑ figure it out using evidence

   Ⓒ get it wrong

   Ⓓ suppose

4. When you *contemplate,* which of the following do you <u>not</u> do?

   Ⓕ be silly

   Ⓖ take your time

   Ⓗ consider carefully

   Ⓙ think seriously

Writing If you forgot a friend's birthday, and then the friend ignored you, what could you *infer?* How did you *infer* this? Be sure to use the word *infer* in your writing.

_____

_____

_____

_____

involve • exclude omit • omission

Use the reproducible definitions on page 169 and the suggestions on page 6 to introduce the words for each day.

DAY 1

involve
(verb) To have something as a necessary part; include. *Winning the championship will **involve** beating every team.*

Ask: *What are the steps **involved** in becoming a winning team?* List on the board steps that students name. (e.g., choosing the team; training; practicing; playing many games) Confirm how each step is a necessary part of becoming champions. Call on students to complete this sentence, "Becoming a winning team **involves** ___." Then have students complete the Day 1 activities on page 51. You may want to do the first one as a group.

DAY 2

involve
(verb) To bring into a situation. *Our teacher **involves** parents as guest speakers on Occupation Day.*

exclude
(verb) To keep or leave something or someone out. *We **exclude** some jobs on Occupation Day because we can't include everything.*

Review the meaning of **involve** from Day 1. Say: ***Involve** can also be used to indicate that someone or something will need to be brought into a situation.* As an example, ask: *Who would you like to **involve** in a discussion on mammals?* (e.g., zoologist; veterinarian) Say: *When you **exclude** someone or something, you leave them out.* Ask: *If we made a list of mammals, what would we **exclude**?* (anything that is not a mammal) Point out that **involve** and **exclude** are antonyms. Then have students complete the Day 2 activities on page 51. You may want to do the first one as a group.

DAY 3

omit
(verb) To leave out; not include. *Let's not **omit** a single event when we describe our fantastic vacation!*

Say: *When you **omit** something, you leave it out.* Ask: *If I circle a sentence in one of your stories and write **omit** next to it, what should you do with that sentence?* (leave it out of your next draft) Then ask: *What would you **omit** from a description of a vacation to keep the story interesting?* Then have students complete the Day 3 activities on page 52. You may want to do the first one as a group.

DAY 4

omission
(noun) Something that is left out, removed, or not done. *It was an **omission** to not give credit to everyone who worked on the project.*

Say: *An **omission** may have a positive or negative result. For example, the **omission** of unnecessary details would make a report more clear. The **omission** of a key ingredient in a recipe would result in a poor-tasting dish.* Invite students to provide their own examples of positive or negative **omissions**. Then have students complete the Day 4 activities on page 52. You may want to do the first one as a group.

DAY 5

Have students complete page 53. Call on students to read aloud their answers to the writing activity.

Daily Academic Vocabulary • EMC 2762 • © Evan-Moor Corp.

Name_____

Daily Academic Vocabulary

Day 1 involve

1. How would you complete this sentence? Say it aloud to a partner.

Doing well in school involves _____.

2. If class reports *involve* doing research, what does that mean? Circle your answer.

    a. Research is not needed for the reports.

    b. The class members are being studied for research.

    c. The reports are about people who do research.

    d. Class members need to do research for their reports.

3. Which word is a synonym for *involve*? Circle your answer.

    a. push

    b. require

    c. find

    d. inspire

Day 2 involve • exclude

1. How would you complete these sentences? Say them aloud to a partner.

I would not want to be involved in _____.

It is rude to exclude _____ from _____.

2. If a friend wants to *involve* you in an activity, what does that mean? Circle your answer.

    a. The friend wants you to be part of the activity.

    b. The friend lives far away from you.

    c. It is necessary for you to do the activity.

    d. The friend is keeping the activity a secret.

3. Which word is a synonym for *exclude*? Circle your answer.

    a. welcome

    b. reject

    c. excite

    d. interest

4. If you needed help on a school project, whom would you *involve*? Why?

_____

_____

Daily Academic Vocabulary

Day 3 | omit

1. How would you complete this sentence? Say it aloud to a partner.

If I could omit one activity from my day, it would be _____.

2. A teacher will *omit* your lowest quiz score when figuring your grade. What should that do to your grade? Circle your answer.

   a. lower your grade
   b. make no difference to your grade
   c. raise your grade
   d. cause you to fail

3. You send in a drawing to an art contest but *omit* the entry form. What did you do? Circle your answer.

   a. You filled out the form incorrectly.
   b. You attached the form in the wrong place.
   c. You sent the form to the wrong address.
   d. You did not include the entry form.

Don't **omit** parrot treats from the shopping list!

Day 4 | omission

1. How would you complete this sentence? Say it aloud to a partner.

Forgetting to _____ is an omission I would never make.

2. A newspaper article about a school event included an *omission*. What happened? Circle your answer.

   a. An important piece of information was not included in the article.
   b. The article was very long.
   c. The article included a quote from the principal.
   d. The school schedule for the year was included in the article.

3. Which sentence uses *omission* correctly? Circle your answer.

   a. The omission needs some ideas to make it clearer.
   b. Please omission some words to make the sentence shorter.
   c. One serious omission in the team list was the name of the coach.
   d. If you need an omission to the report, you can add some artwork.

Day 5 involve • exclude • omit • omission

Fill in the bubble next to the correct answer.

1. Which of these does a group project <u>not</u> involve?

Ⓐ sharing ideas with others

Ⓑ team planning

Ⓒ sharing responsibilities

Ⓓ being best friends

2. In which sentence could *exclude* replace the underlined word(s)?

Ⓕ We can <u>invite</u> more friends to have a bigger party.

Ⓖ Everyone should try to <u>contribute</u> food and games.

Ⓗ The party will be better if we <u>keep out</u> troublemakers.

Ⓙ We need helpers to <u>clean out</u> the basement for the party.

3. In which sentence could the word *omit* fill in the blank?

Ⓐ We need to _____ one player because we have too many today.

Ⓑ We need to _____ one player because we have too few today.

Ⓒ We need to _____ the team to get started.

Ⓓ We need to _____ the game and continue when it stops raining.

4. Which word is an antonym for *omission*?

Ⓕ deletion

Ⓖ addition

Ⓗ opportunity

Ⓙ error

Writing   What steps would be *involved* in starting a club? Explain your ideas.
Be sure to use the word *involve* in your writing.

_____

_____

_____

_____

former • latter

Use the reproducible definitions on page 170 and the suggestions on page 6 to introduce the words for each day.

DAY 1

former
(noun) The first of two things mentioned. *Between the first-grade teacher and the fifth-grade teacher, the **former** has been teaching longer.*

Hold up two books. Say: *I have two choices of what to read. This is one choice.* Hold up one book. *This book is the other choice.* Hold up the other book. *I choose to read the **former**. Which is my choice?* (the first book) Repeat with different pairs (e.g., paper, chalk; chalk, book) for students to practice identifying the **former** of two things. Point out that "the" is used before **former** as a noun. Then have students complete the Day 1 activities on page 55. You may want to do the first one as a group.

DAY 2

former
(adj.) Having to do with the past; previous. *The **former** principal of our school returned to receive an award.*

Explain that **former** has two meanings, one a noun and the other an adjective. Ask students to name some of their **former** teachers, using the word **former**. Say: *Note that some of your **former** teachers are still teaching, but they are no longer teaching you. They were your teachers in the past.* Then have students complete the Day 2 activities on page 55. You may want to do the first one as a group.

DAY 3

latter
(noun) The second of two things mentioned. *We will visit a museum and an aquarium, but we are more excited about the **latter** because we love fish!*

Review what students learned about "former" on Day 1. Repeat the demonstrations from Day 1, emphasizing the second choice of each pair, to explain the meaning of **latter**. Say: *I choose the **latter**. Which is my choice?* Encourage students to use the word **latter** in their responses. Then have students complete the Day 3 activities on page 56. You may want to do the first one as a group.

DAY 4

latter
(adj.) Near the end. *The **latter** part of the book, after the hero is captured, is the most exciting to read.*

Say: *Like "former," the word **latter** has two meanings, one a noun and one an adjective. **Latter** as an adjective is often used with the word "part" to show that something is nearer the end than the beginning.* Have students describe events that take place in the **latter** part of their school day. Then have students complete the Day 4 activities on page 56. You may want to do the first one as a group.

DAY 5

Have students complete page 57. Call on students to read aloud their answers to the writing activity.

Day 1 **former**

1. How would you complete this sentence? Say it aloud to a partner.

If I have a choice to _____ or to _____, I usually choose the former.

2. You read an article that compares India and China for a report you are doing on the *former*. What is the subject of your report? Circle your answer.

    a. China

    b. India

    c. both China and India

    d. Asia

3. Which of these would help you identify the *former* of two songs sung at a concert? Circle your answer.

    a. having the words to the songs in front of you

    b. knowing which song your friends like

    c. knowing when the concert started and finished

    d. having a program that lists the order of the songs

Day 2 **former**

1. How would you complete this sentence? Say it aloud to a partner.

A former _____ of mine that I admire is _____.

2. A guest speaker is introduced as the city's *former* police chief. Which of these is true of the guest? Circle your answer.

    a. The guest is currently the city's police chief.

    b. The guest is currently the city's fire chief.

    c. The guest is no longer the city's police chief.

    d. The guest can no longer speak.

3. Which word is a synonym for *former*? Circle your answer.

    a. past

    b. friendly

    c. modern

    d. famous

My **former** home was South America.

Daily
Academic
Vocabulary

Day 3 latter

1. **How would you complete this sentence? Say it aloud to a partner.**

   Between fall and spring, many people prefer the latter because _____ is _____.

2. **Which of these is always true of the *latter* of two choices? Circle your answer.**

   a. It's the best choice.
   b. It's smaller than the other choice.
   c. It's not the first of the choices.
   d. It's the only choice.

3. **At lunch you have an apple and a banana. Your friend wants the *latter* and trades an orange for it. What fruits do you have now? Circle your answer.**

   a. apple and banana   c. banana and orange
   b. apple and orange   d. apple, banana, and orange

Day 4 latter

1. **How would you complete this sentence? Say it aloud to a partner.**

   A holiday that falls in the latter part of the year is _____.

2. **You turn on the television and find a channel playing the *latter* part of a movie you like. What does that mean? Circle your answer.**

   a. The movie has just ended.
   b. The movie is just starting.
   c. Less than half of the movie has been shown.
   d. More than half of the movie has been shown.

3. **Your history teacher says a quiz will cover the *latter* events in the life of a famous president. How should you prepare for the quiz? Circle your answer.**

   a. Review every event of his life.
   b. Review the earliest events of his life.
   c. Review events near the end of his life.
   d. Review events that happened after he died.

4. **Write about what you did in the *latter* part of your summer vacation.**

   _____

   _____

Name_____

Day 5 **former • latter**

Fill in the bubble next to the correct answer.

1. Which sentence uses *former* correctly?

   Ⓐ Between winter and spring, the former is spring.

   Ⓑ Every season comes former than the other.

   Ⓒ Between summer and winter, the former is the hotter time of year.

   Ⓓ Summer seems former every year.

2. In which sentence could *former* replace the underlined word?

   Ⓕ The <u>new</u> school is opening this week.

   Ⓖ Our <u>previous</u> school was built years ago.

   Ⓗ The <u>biggest</u> school is the high school.

   Ⓙ A <u>future</u> school may have no classrooms at all.

3. In which sentence could *latter* fill in the blank?

   Ⓐ The two puppies were born in the _____ basket.

   Ⓑ I was shown two puppies, Roscoe and Chloe, and I chose the _____.

   Ⓒ The _____ of puppies have not been born yet.

   Ⓓ One puppy was born _____ than the others.

4. Which word is an antonym for *latter*?

   Ⓕ earlier

   Ⓖ later

   Ⓗ second

   Ⓙ farther

Writing   Describe one of your favorite *former* teachers or coaches.
Be sure to use the word *former* in your writing.

_____

_____

_____

_____

manner • system • systematic

Use the reproducible definitions on page 171 and the suggestions on page 6 to introduce the words for each day.

DAY 1

manner
(noun) A way of doing things; style. *The careful manner in which Harris always completes his homework impresses his teacher.*

Say: ***Manner** is a general way of describing how someone does things. You need more information to know about the particular **manner** in which things are done.* Have students complete this sentence: "My **manner** of preparing for a test is to ___." Then have students complete the Day 1 activities on page 59. You may want to do the first one as a group.

DAY 2

system
(noun) A group of related things or parts that work together as a whole. *The computer system stopped working when the electricity went off.*

Discuss the parts that make up a computer **system**. (e.g., computers and printers that are linked together) Ask: *What makes those parts a **system**?* (they work together to form a whole) Then ask: *What other types of **systems** have you heard about?* (e.g., solar **system**; subway **system**) Then have students complete the Day 2 activities on page 59. You may want to do the first one as a group.

DAY 3

system
(noun) A particular way or method of doing something. *Arianna needs a better system for remembering her homework, because she often forgets to bring it to school.*

Say: ***System** also can mean a particular way to do something. Its meaning is similar to "manner," but **system** is often used when the way in which things are done follows a plan or method.* Then refer to the sample sentence. Ask: *Can you think of a **system** for remembering to bring your homework to school?* (e.g., place it by the door at night) Then have students complete the Day 3 activities on page 60. You may want to do the first one as a group.

DAY 4

systematic
(adj.) Involving or based on a method or plan. *A more systematic way to organize our class library would be to arrange the books by subject matter.*

Point out that **systematic** is related to the meaning of "system" that was covered on Day 3. Say: *When something involves a specific method or plan, or is done in a certain way, we say that it is **systematic**.* Ask: *What makes arranging books by subject matter a **systematic** way to organize books?* (e.g., it's a logical method) Have students think of other ways to organize a library in a **systematic** way. (e.g., arrange them alphabetically by title or author; Dewey Decimal System) Then have students complete the Day 4 activities on page 60. You may want to do the first one as a group.

DAY 5

Have students complete page 61. Call on students to read aloud their answers to the writing activity.

Name_____

Day 1 | manner

1. How would you complete this sentence? Say it aloud to a partner.

My usual manner of greeting someone is to say _____.

2. Which word is a synonym for *manner?* Circle your answer.

a. polite   c. way

b. exhibit   d. subject

3. Your teacher announces that her *manner* of assigning homework will change. What does that mean? Circle your answer.

a. The class will no longer receive any homework.

b. The way that homework assignments are given will change.

c. The class will receive less homework.

d. How students complete their homework will need to change.

Day 2 | system

1. How would you complete this sentence? Say it aloud to a partner.

Another school in our school system is _____.

2. You are studying a *system* in the human body. What are you learning? Circle your answer.

a. how specific parts of the body work together

b. how to get along better with others

c. how people look and act alike or different

d. how to improve your study skills

3. Which phrase is not related to the idea of a *system?* Circle your answer.

a. being connected

b. working together

c. consisting of several parts

d. working independently

4. Why is the solar *system* a *system?*

I use my muscular **system** to ride my bike.

_____

_____

Day 3 | system

1. How would you complete this sentence? Say it aloud to a partner.

Our teacher's system for checking attendance is _____.

2. In which sentence is *system* <u>not</u> used correctly? Circle your answer.

a. Voting is one system for choosing leaders.

b. Every library has a system for organizing materials.

c. A principal is a system for leading a school.

d. Our coach's training system helps us get in shape.

3. Which word is a synonym for *system?* Circle your answer.

a. method   c. product

b. setting   d. operation

Day 4 | systematic

1. How would you complete this sentence? Say it aloud to a partner.

A systematic way to clean up my room would be to _____.

2. Which word would <u>not</u> describe something that is *systematic?* Circle your answer.

a. planned   c. careless

b. methodical   d. consistent

**3. A school has a *systematic* approach to fire drills. What does that mean?
Circle your answer.**

a. The school has not planned for fire drills.

b. The school follows a specific plan for fire drills.

c. The school has evidence of a serious fire.

d. The school is down the street from the fire department.

4. Describe something you do in a *systematic* way.

_____

_____

_____

Name_____

Day 5 **manner • system • systematic**

Fill in the bubble next to the correct answer.

1. In which sentence could *manner* be used to fill in the blank?

 Ⓐ They talked too loudly and showed terrible _____.

 Ⓑ We discussed the _____ together.

 Ⓒ Her _____ of working with others is to ask for their ideas.

 Ⓓ We can work together to find a _____ for this problem.

2. In which sentence is *system* <u>not</u> used correctly?

 Ⓕ They should work together to system their ideas.

 Ⓖ There is a system of pipes for carrying water.

 Ⓗ A car is an elaborate mechanical system.

 Ⓙ A telephone system can connect people around the world.

3. In which sentence could *system* replace the underlined word?

 Ⓐ The project <u>goal</u> is to build a working battery.

 Ⓑ The main <u>problem</u> is not having enough materials.

 Ⓒ The only <u>solution</u> is to change projects.

 Ⓓ We need a better <u>way</u> for how we choose projects.

4. In which sentence is *systematic* used correctly?

 Ⓕ Hector's teacher was systematic to his problems.

 Ⓖ A systematic program will be well thought out.

 Ⓗ The ideas will be connected as a systematic.

 Ⓙ Olivia was systematic because she never did things the same way.

Writing   Describe your *system* for doing homework. Be sure to use the word *system* in your writing.

_____

_____

_____

_____

strategy • strategize procedure • method

Use the reproducible definitions on page 172 and the suggestions on page 6 to introduce the words for each day.

DAY 1

strategy
(noun) A careful plan or method for achieving a goal. *The student's* **strategy** *for winning the reading contest is to read a book every day.*

Check for students' familiarity with **strategy** from instruction in various subjects. Say: *We use* **strategies** *to learn at school.* Ask: *What are the* **strategies** *we use to solve a word problem in math? When you read, what are some* **strategies** *you use to remember important ideas?* Encourage students to use the word **strategy** in their responses. Then have students complete the Day 1 activities on page 63. You may want to do the first one as a group.

DAY 2

strategize
(verb) To plan or decide on a strategy. *Our science team* **strategized** *on how to finish our project on time.*

Say: *We can* **strategize** *many things. I* **strategize** *how to teach every day. You often* **strategize** *in school.* Ask: *How do you* **strategize** *to finish projects or assignments on time?* (e.g., prioritize what needs to be done and assign roles) Then discuss other situations that might require students to **strategize**. (e.g., how to juggle after-school activities) Have students complete the Day 2 activities on page 63. You may want to do the first one as a group.

DAY 3

procedure
(noun) A way of doing something following an orderly series of steps. *The students learned the fire-safety* **procedure** *of stop, drop, and roll.*

Refer to the sample sentence and ask: *What makes stop, drop, and roll a* **procedure**? (e.g., follow the steps in a certain order) Have students describe other safety **procedures**. (e.g., fire drills; earthquake drills; stop-look-listen) Say: *We also follow* **procedures** *for many of our everyday activities at school.* Have students name some of these **procedures** and describe the steps that are followed. Then have students complete the Day 3 activities on page 64. You may want to do the first one as a group.

DAY 4

method
(noun) A way in which something is done. *One* **method** *of learning new words is to make flashcards.*

Say: *A* **method** *is anything that you do in a certain way. It is more general than a strategy, which is a careful way of achieving a goal, or a procedure, that follows an orderly series of steps. We each have our own* **methods** *that we follow.* Ask: *What are your* **methods** *of studying?* See how many different **methods** the students describe. Then have students complete the Day 4 activities on page 64. You may want to do the first one as a group.

DAY 5

Have students complete page 65. Call on students to read aloud their answers to the writing activity.

Name_____

Day 1 **strategy**

1. How would you complete this sentence? Say it aloud to a partner.

A good strategy for getting along with others at school is _____.

2. If you learn a math *strategy* to use in solving word problems, what have you learned? Circle your answer.

    a. why math is hard for some students

    b. some new numbers

    c. a plan for solving word problems

    d. a word problem to solve

3. Which sentence uses *strategy* correctly? Circle your answer.

    a. The coach has several good players to strategy.

    b. We can strategy together after the game.

    c. Our best strategy is sick today with a cold.

    d. We have a strategy for winning this game.

4. Describe a *strategy* you could follow to read more books in a year.

_____

Day 2 **strategize**

1. How would you complete this sentence? Say it aloud to a partner.

My friends and I sometimes strategize on how to _____.

2. To raise money for a trip, your class needs to *strategize*. What does that mean? Circle your answer.

    a. The class needs to give up on taking the trip.

    b. The class needs to come up with ways to raise money.

    c. The class needs to choose a place to go on a trip.

    d. The class needs to find parents who will go with them.

3. Which of these would most likely require you to *strategize*? Circle your answer.

    a. eating dinner

    b. sharpening your pencil

    c. completing a group project

    d. sitting at your desk

I need to **strategize** on how to get more peanuts.

Day 3 procedure

1. How would you complete this sentence? Say it aloud to a partner.

My procedure for doing my homework is to start by _____.

2. Which word is not a synonym for *procedure*? Circle your answer.

    a. confusion   c. method

    b. process   d. approach

3. If you follow a *procedure* to check out books from the library, which of these is true? Circle your answer.

    a. You do something different each time you check out a book.

    b. There is a set of steps to follow to check out a book.

    c. You can check out only one book at a time.

    d. You must promise to check out books from the library.

4. Write about a new *procedure* you learned this year.

_____

_____

Day 4 method

1. How would you complete this sentence? Say it aloud to a partner.

The method I use for studying new words is _____.

2. Based on what you know, how would you define "scientific *method*"? Circle your answer.

    a. what helps you remember how to spell "scientific"

    b. how you make science

    c. the way that people study and learn about science

    d. doing science for a method

3. If someone tells you there are three possible *methods* for constructing a model bridge, what does that mean? Circle your answer.

    a. You can construct the bridge in only one way.

    b. You can build the bridge however you choose.

    c. The bridge cannot be built for three reasons.

    d. There are three ways you can build the bridge.

Name_____

Daily Academic Vocabulary

Fill in the bubble next to the correct answer.

1. In which sentence could the word *strategy* fill in the blank?

Ⓐ This week we will _____ in basketball practice.

Ⓑ A reading _____ will help me comprehend better.

Ⓒ The test will be on the _____ of science.

Ⓓ A history text provides a _____ of events.

2. In which sentence could *strategize* replace the underlined words?

Ⓕ We need a <u>list of ideas</u> for a class play.

Ⓖ Our <u>purpose</u> is to include everyone in a production.

Ⓗ We <u>can include everyone</u> in making costumes and scenery.

Ⓙ We should <u>develop a plan</u> to be sure everyone has a role.

3. Which sentence does <u>not</u> describe part of a *procedure*?

Ⓐ We start the recipe by cooking some eggs and then adding milk.

Ⓑ The next step in locking up the room is to close all the windows.

Ⓒ After I go to the store, I don't know what I will be doing next.

Ⓓ The fire drill ends with all students returning to their classrooms.

4. Which word is a synonym for *method*?

Ⓕ way

Ⓖ kind

Ⓗ revision

Ⓙ retreat

Writing   Describe the *procedure* that is followed during a *Daily Academic Vocabulary* lesson. Be sure to use at least one of this week's words in your writing.

_____

_____

_____

_____

account • account for • version

Use the reproducible definitions on page 173 and the suggestions on page 6 to introduce the words for each day.

DAY 1

account
(noun) A written or spoken description of something that has happened. *Each student will give an **account** of the class field trip.*

Ask: *What would you include in an **account** of a field trip?* (e.g., where you went; what you saw; what you learned) Have students give **accounts** of a recent field trip, assembly, or other school event. Then have students complete the Day 1 activities on page 67. You may want to do the first one as a group.

DAY 2

account for
(verb) To explain. *We can **account for** the missing equipment, which was loaned to another team.*

Write "**account for**" on the board. Ask: *How can you use what you learned about "account" as a clue to the meaning of **account for**?* (e.g., it has to do with describing or explaining something that happened) Ask: *If you had to **account for** missing homework, what would you need to do?* (e.g., explain where the homework is or why it isn't done) Then have students complete the Day 2 activities on page 67. You may want to do the first one as a group.

DAY 3

version
(noun) A description or account from a particular point of view. *Each child had a different **version** of how the window was broken.*

Refer to the sample sentence. Call on a student and say: *(Student's name), I want you to role-play as the person who broke the window. Can you give me your **version** of how it happened?* Then call on another student to role-play and ask for his or her **version** of the same event. Discuss how the two descriptions of what happened might be similar or different, but how each is the individual's **version**, or view, of events. Then have students complete the Day 3 activities on page 68. You may want to do the first one as a group.

DAY 4

version
(noun) A changed or different form of something. *Adam chose to include a pink rose instead of a red rose in his **version** of the flower painting.*

Explain that similar things in different forms are called **versions**. Ask: *Can you name a movie that is based on a book?* (e.g., *Charlotte's Web; Hoot*) *Which **version** did you like better, the book **version** or the movie **version**? These are both **versions** because they are different forms of the same story.* Note that a **version** can be very similar to or very different from the original, depending on the changes. Then have students complete the Day 4 activities on page 68. You may want to do the first one as a group.

DAY 5

Have students complete page 69. Call on students to read aloud their answers to the writing activity.

Name_____

Day 1 account

1. How would you complete this sentence? Say it aloud to a partner.

An account of my family's best vacation would include _____.

2. Your parent wants an *account* of your after-school activities. What do you need to provide? Circle your answer.

    a. how much you spend on snacks
    b. a teacher's signature on your homework
    c. a description of what you did after school
    d. evidence that you go to school

3. You are to read an *account* of a person's trip to another country. Which of these would you <u>not</u> expect to learn? Circle your answer.

    a. details about what happened on the trip
    b. what the person's life is like at home
    c. information on the places that the person visited
    d. how the person felt about the trip

I will write an **account** of my rainforest adventure.

Day 2 account for

1. How would you complete this sentence? Say it aloud to a partner.

I had to account for my whereabouts when _____.

2. Your teacher asks you to *account for* a math error you made. What do you need to do? Circle your answer.

    a. do extra work to make up for a bad grade
    b. correct the error you made
    c. count the number of math errors you have made lately
    d. explain why you think you made the error

3. Which sentence uses *account for* correctly? Circle your answer.

    a. Our team needs to account for why we lost the game.
    b. If we had an account for the game, we would win.
    c. Let's invite the winners to account for us.
    d. When there is an account for winning, everyone is happy.

4. How could you *account for* a lost pencil?

_____

Day 3 version

1. **How would you complete this sentence? Say it aloud to a partner.**

   A friend and I once gave different versions of how _____.

2. **You are reading a character's *version* of an event in a story. What does that mean? Circle your answer.**

   a. You are getting the character's description of the event.
   b. No one in the story knows about the event.
   c. The story is about an event that really happened.
   d. You are reading a description of the character.

3. **Which phrase would not be used to describe two people's *versions* of an event that took place two years ago? Circle your answer.**

   a. similar in most respects   c. completely identical
   b. different in some details   d. mostly the same

Day 4 version

1. **How would you complete this sentence? Say it aloud to a partner.**

   I have heard different versions of the song "_____."

2. **Which statement explains how to make a new *version* of your favorite sandwich? Circle your answer.**

   a. Make the exact same sandwich you always make.
   b. Make another kind of sandwich and not your favorite sandwich.
   c. Don't make a sandwich at all.
   d. Make your favorite sandwich but use a new kind of bread.

3. **A particular movie is a *version* of a popular book. What does that mean? Circle your answer.**

   a. The movie is not as popular as the book.
   b. The movie is based on the book but is different in some ways.
   c. The movie is boring.
   d. The movie is more fun to watch than reading the book.

4. **Write a two-sentence *version* of a fairy tale.**

   _____

   _____

Name_____

Day 5 | account • account for • version

Fill in the bubble next to the correct answer.

1. Which word is a synonym for *account*?

Ⓐ report

Ⓑ problem

Ⓒ pattern

Ⓓ dream

2. Which of these describes what you are doing when you *account for* your behavior?

Ⓕ trying to control your behavior

Ⓖ promising to improve your behavior

Ⓗ giving an explanation of your behavior

Ⓘ learning new behavior

3. In which sentence could *version* fill in the blank?

Ⓐ The _____ to this problem is hard to find.

Ⓑ That event would make a good _____ in a movie.

Ⓒ We can _____ the story to make it more interesting.

Ⓓ His _____ of the accident was different from mine.

4. To create a *version* of something, what do you need to do?

Ⓕ ruin it

Ⓖ change it

Ⓗ clean it

Ⓘ count it

Writing   Give an *account* of a recent activity you enjoyed doing. Use at least one of this week's words in your writing.

_____

_____

_____

_____

analyze • analysis
classify • classification

Use the reproducible definitions on page 174 and the suggestions on page 6 to introduce the words for each day.

DAY 1

analyze
(verb) To examine something in great detail in order to understand it. *The teacher will analyze the test results to determine what skills students need help on.*

Say: *When you analyze something, you look closely at all its parts or pieces in order to understand it better. For example, when we analyze a math word problem, what do we look at?* (e.g., question being asked; information and figures given) *If we analyze the results of a science experiment, what would we do?* (e.g., decide what the results showed; determine if the question was answered) Then have students complete the Day 1 activities on page 71. You may want to do the first one as a group.

DAY 2

analysis
(noun) A careful study of the parts of something in order to better understand the whole. *The principal's analysis of the new rules showed that they help students get along better.*

Say: *When you analyze something, you do an analysis of it. For example, you might analyze how your grades have changed over the years. This would be an analysis of your report cards.* Discuss examples of *analysis* that students do in school. (e.g., study stories to identify their themes; study a character's actions) Then have students complete the Day 2 activities on page 71. You may want to do the first one as a group.

DAY 3

classify
(verb) To put things into groups based on their characteristics. *We can classify our family's pets into two groups—those with fur and those with feathers.*

Gather several books and writing tools. Say: *I want to group these objects. I will classify them into two groups: "things to read" and "things to write with."* Put one item in the wrong group. Ask: *Have I classified these objects correctly?* (No) *Which object have I not correctly classified?* Then ask: *When have you classified things?* (e.g., science; collections) Then have students complete the Day 3 activities on page 72. You may want to do the first one as a group.

DAY 4

classification
(noun) An arrangement of things into groups based on their characteristics. *One simple classification of books is fiction and nonfiction.*

Say: *When you classify objects, you put them into classifications.* Refer to the sample sentence. Say: *This is a basic classification. It puts all books into two groups—those that are stories in fiction and those that aren't in nonfiction.* Ask students to suggest a further **classification** of fiction books. (e.g., by author; by type of story; by length) Then have students complete the Day 4 activities on page 72. You may want to do the first one as a group.

DAY 5

Have students complete page 73. Call on students to read aloud their answers to the writing activity.

Name_____

Day 1 analyze

1. How would you complete this sentence? Say it aloud to a partner.

I would need help if I had to analyze _____.

2. Which word is not a synonym for *analyze*? Circle your answer.

   a. investigate   c. imitate

   b. evaluate   d. examine

3. Which of these would best help you to *analyze* why two friends are not getting along? Circle your answer.

   a. talking to both friends to get their points of view

   b. siding with one friend against the other

   c. trying not to learn too much about why they are not getting along

   d. telling the friends to shake hands and make up

4. Name something you think would be interesting to *analyze*. How could you *analyze* it?

_____

Day 2 analysis

1. How would you complete this sentence? Say it aloud to a partner.

An analysis of my typical day would show that I spend a lot of time _____.

2. Which sentence uses *analysis* correctly? Circle your answer.

   a. The scientist made an analysis that blew up in the lab.

   b. The analysis of the story included descriptions of the main characters.

   c. The teacher will analysis our grades to decide if we need more homework.

   d. The country's big events will be analysis in the future.

3. A coach asks team members to do an *analysis* of a winning game. Which of these would not be part of the process? Circle your answer.

   a. identifying examples of teamwork in the game

   b. identifying good plays in the game

   c. identifying bad plays in the game

   d. identifying players for next year's team

An **analysis** of the moon will reveal its effects on the tides.

Name _____

Day 3 classify

1. **How would you complete this sentence? Say it aloud to a partner.**

   Something that people classify by size is _____.

2. **Describe three ways to *classify* different kinds of sports.**

   a. _____

   b. _____

   c. _____

3. **Which of these would you not need to do to *classify* a set of objects by the sounds they make? Circle your answer.**

   a. listen to the objects
   b. group the objects by type of sound
   c. identify the objects that have similar sounds
   d. choose the objects that have similar shapes

Day 4 classification

1. **How would you complete this sentence? Say it aloud to a partner.**

   _____ and _____ are two foods that fall under the classification of _____.

2. **Which of these would be most helpful in the *classification* of plants? Circle your answer.**

   a. observing plants to identify their characteristics
   b. watering them on a regular basis
   c. observing different insects that live on plants
   d. planting seeds to grow a garden

3. **An exhibit on the *classification* of butterflies would focus on which of the following? Circle your answer.**

   a. how to grow a garden that attracts butterflies
   b. how a caterpillar becomes a butterfly
   c. butterflies' different colors, sizes, and patterns on their wings
   d. why butterflies are popular insects

The **classification** of birds is based on genetic similarities.

BIG BIRD BOOK

Day 5 analyze • analysis • classify • classification

Fill in the bubble next to the correct answer.

1. Which of these are the most important skills to use when you *analyze*?

Ⓐ teaching skills

Ⓑ thinking skills

Ⓒ cooking skills

Ⓓ art skills

2. In which sentence could *analysis* be used to fill in the blank?

Ⓕ The class is doing an experiment and then will _____ the results.

Ⓖ Keeping _____ during the experiment will help us write our report.

Ⓗ The main purpose of the experiment is to test for _____.

Ⓙ An _____ of the experiment showed a different result than the class expected.

3. Which word describes what you do when you *classify*?

Ⓐ multiply

Ⓑ copy

Ⓒ organize

Ⓓ exclaim

4. Which of these would <u>not</u> be used in the *classification* of animals?

Ⓕ how they move

Ⓖ what they eat

Ⓗ where they live

Ⓙ what they think about

Writing   Describe a way in which you could *classify* the different books that you have read. Use at least one of this week's words in your writing.

_____

_____

_____

_____

acquire • accumulate
accumulation • compile

Use the reproducible definitions on page 175 and the suggestions on page 6 to introduce the words for each day.

DAY 1

acquire
(verb) To get as your own. *I just **acquired** a new bike.*

Refer to the sample sentence. Ask: *How could you **acquire** a bike?* (e.g., buy one; be given a hand-me-down) Say: *You can **acquire** objects such as a bike. What can you **acquire** that is <u>not</u> an object?* (e.g., friendships; knowledge; skills) Ask: *How do students **acquire** knowledge and skills in school?* (e.g., through study; practice; working hard) Then have students complete the Day 1 activities on page 75. You may want to do the first one as a group.

DAY 2

accumulate
(verb) To collect, gather together, or let pile up. *I will **accumulate** many rocks in order to build a wall.*

Say: *Imagine that the custodians were sick for a week. What would happen?* (e.g., papers and other trash would pile up) Explain that the trash would **accumulate**. Say: *Sometimes people want to **accumulate** things.* Ask students to think of something that they may have **accumulated**. (e.g., card collections; games) Then have students complete the Day 2 activities on page 75. You may want to do the first one as a group.

DAY 3

accumulation
(noun) An amount that collects or piles up. *There is an **accumulation** of empty bottles in the garage.*

Say: *If objects are allowed to accumulate, we are left with an **accumulation** of those objects. For example, if it snows all night, the snow will accumulate and we will see an **accumulation** of snow on the ground when we look out the window in the morning.* Have students name other things of which there can be an **accumulation**. (e.g., toys; leaves in the yard; old newspapers; dust on undusted surfaces) Then have students complete the Day 3 activities on page 76. You may want to do the first one as a group.

DAY 4

compile
(verb) To collect or put together in an orderly form. *We should **compile** the list of sources that we used for our report.*

Start a class list as an example for **compile**. Call on a few students to say their favorite colors as you write their names and favorite colors on the board. Confirm that you gathered information (names and colors) to **compile** a list. Ask: *How do you **compile** sources for reports?* (e.g., list books and Web sites) Then have students complete the Day 4 activities on page 76. You may want to do the first one as a group.

DAY 5

Have students complete page 77. Call on students to read aloud their answers to the writing activity.

Name_____

Day 1 acquire

1. How would you complete this sentence? Say it aloud to a partner.

Something I would like my family to acquire is _____.

2. Students must *acquire* a uniform for school. What does that mean? Circle your answer.

    a. Every student is against uniforms.

    b. Students want to dress the same.

    c. Every student must get a school uniform.

    d. Students will come to school in one group.

3. Which of these would help you most to *acquire* a particular skill? Circle your answer.

    a. having a friend with this skill

    b. learning and practicing the skill yourself

    c. watching your teacher use the skill

    d. hearing about what you can do with this skill

4. Name something you recently *acquired*. How did you *acquire* it?

_____

Day 2 accumulate

1. How would you complete this sentence? Say it aloud to a partner.

Something that can accumulate on the ground is _____.

2. Emma spends a week at the beach and *accumulates* seashells. What does that mean? Circle your answer.

    a. She throws away all the seashells she finds.

    b. She buries many seashells on the beach.

    c. She sells many seashells at the beach.

    d. She finds and collects many seashells.

3. You need to *accumulate* information for a report. What do you need to do? Circle your answer.

    a. gather information to use in the report

    b. throw out information you don't need

    c. collect reports

    d. think of a topic for a report

I never let my feathers **accumulate** dust!

Day 3 | accumulation

1. How would you complete this sentence? Say it aloud to a partner.

In my room I have an accumulation of _____.

2. Which word would <u>not</u> be used to describe an *accumulation*? Circle your answer.

  a. growing   c. friendly

  b. increasing   d. large

3. Juana has an *accumulation* of newspaper. Which sentence best explains why she has an *accumulation*? Circle your answer.

  a. She picked up her neighbor's newspaper this morning.

  b. She kept every day's newspaper for a month.

  c. She gave many newspapers away.

  d. She asked for a job at a newspaper.

Day 4 | compile

1. How would you complete this sentence? Say it aloud to a partner.

Something that a family might compile is _____.

2. Which word is a synonym for *compile*? Circle your answer.

  a. sort   c. assemble

  b. write   d. edit

3. Your teacher asks you to *compile* a list of materials needed for the science experiment. What do you need to do? Circle your answer.

  a. Make labels for the equipment.

  b. Write down the name of each item needed.

  c. Look in the cupboard.

  d. Do the experiment.

4. What questions would you *compile* before interviewing a famous artist? List three.

_____

_____

_____

Name _____

Day 5 | acquire • accumulate
accumulation • compile

Fill in the bubble next to the correct answer.

1. Which sentence uses *acquire* correctly?

Ⓐ I have to acquire an illness for school.

Ⓑ I need to acquire a library card to check out books.

Ⓒ Hannah wants to acquire herself in a new dress.

Ⓓ There is one acquire that all students must meet.

2. In which sentence could *accumulate* fill in the blank?

Ⓕ It would be fun to _____ exhibits at the museum.

Ⓖ It would be fun to _____ stars on a summer night.

Ⓗ It would be fun to _____ rare baseball cards.

Ⓙ It would be fun to _____ a party for all of my friends.

3. Which word would <u>not</u> be used as a synonym for *accumulation*?

Ⓐ invitation

Ⓑ pile

Ⓒ stack

Ⓓ collection

4. Which sentence does <u>not</u> use *compile* correctly?

Ⓕ We can compile our stories into a book.

Ⓖ We need to compile a list of camping supplies.

Ⓗ We can go to the market to compile our dinner.

Ⓙ We have a week to compile the information.

Writing Explain a good way to *acquire* information about a subject that interests you. Be sure to use the word *acquire* in your writing.

_____

_____

_____

_____

CUMULATIVE REVIEW
WORDS FROM WEEKS 10–17

account
account for
accumulate
accumulation
acquire
analysis
analyze
classification
classify
compile
contemplate
exclude
former
infer
inference
involve
latter
manner
method
omission
omit
procedure
strategize
strategy
surmise
system
systematic
version

Days 1–4

Each day's activity is a cloze paragraph that students complete with words or forms of words that they have learned in weeks 10–17. Before students begin, pronounce each word in the box on the student page, have students repeat each word, and then review each word's meaning(s). **Other ways to review the words:**

- Start a sentence containing one of the words and have students finish the sentence orally. For example:

    *A dangerous **omission** in a car would be…*
    *Doing the research for a report **involves**…*

- Provide students with a definition and ask them to supply the word that fits it.

- Ask questions that require students to know the meaning of each word. For example:

    *Which **former** president would you like to meet?*
    *What is a **systematic** way to study vocabulary?*

- Have students use each word in a sentence.

Day 5

Start by reviewing the eight words not practiced on Days 1–4: **accumulation, analysis, contemplate, inference, method, procedure, strategize, surmise**. Write the words on the board and have students repeat them after you. Provide a sentence for one of the words. Ask students to think of their own sentence and share it with a partner. Call on several students to share their sentences. Follow the same procedure for the remaining words. Then have students complete the code-breaker activity.

Extension Ideas

Use any of the following activities to help integrate the vocabulary words into other content areas:

- Have students create their own **systematic** method for organizing their notes in history or science.

- Have students identify **systems** in the human body. Have them **classify** organs by **system** and use the **classification** to **account for** why some organs are more important than others for health and life.

- Have students read **accounts** of survival from history or literature. Have students **analyze** the stories for examples of **strategies** that people use to adapt, such as **accumulating** food and supplies, and **acquiring** objects to use as tools or weapons. Have students identify **inferences** they can make about how people survive against the odds.

        Daily Academic Vocabulary • EMC 2762 • © Evan-Moor Corp.

Daily
Academic
Vocabulary

| accumulates | classifications | excludes | latter | omission |
| acquiring | classified | former | manner | strategy |

Day 1

Fill in the blanks with words from the word box.

What do pencils and diamonds have in common? Although people write with

the _____ and wear the _____, both a pencil "lead"

and a diamond are made of pure carbon. Carbon, the sixth element on the periodic

chart, is _____ as a nonmetal. It is a basic building block in over

10 million organisms and substances! In a pencil "lead," the carbon atoms group together

in layers. When carbon piles up and _____ deep underground, the

atoms group together in cubes and form diamonds. With the help of diamond's plain

gray-black cousin, you can create writing that sparkles!

Day 2

Fill in the blanks with words from the word box.

We have two _____ for players on our volleyball team,

beginning and advanced. My coach thinks I might have a chance to play with the

advanced players this year if I use a _____ of consistent practice and

effort. I'm already working on _____ more skills, such as a stronger

serve. I am working on my _____ of cooperation with other players,

too. My coach told me that it's often the _____ of team spirit and lack

of effort that _____ players from moving up to the advanced team.

I am going to work as hard as I can!

Name _____

| account | analyzed | infer | omitted | systematic |
| account for | compiled | involved | system | version |

Day 3

Fill in the blanks with words from the word box.

Tracking was my favorite part of outdoor science camp. We had to use facts and

observations to _____ what kind of animal made the track. One of the

ways we _____ a track was to count the number of toes the animal had.

Then we measured the length and depth of the track. Other information was gathered

in a _____ way and _____ in lists. This included the

direction the track was going and what animals lived in the area. However, sometimes

factors such as rain would _____ us not finding many tracks.

Day 4

Fill in the blanks with words from the word box.

Naomi and her younger sister, Alicia, each wrote an _____ of their

trip to Puerto Rico. Naomi described the bustling capital city, San Juan, and the island's

public transportation _____. Traveling _____

small vans and winding roads as opposed to the buses and freeways at home. Alicia's

_____ of the trip included details about the delicious fried banana-like

plantains and the diversity of marine life. She didn't want to remember the winding roads,

so she _____ that part from her description. Both girls were able to

practice their Spanish and have fun!

Name_____

Day 5

Crack the Code!

Write one of the words from the word box on the lines next to each clue.

account	analyze	former	method	strategy
account for	classification	infer	omission	surmise
accumulate	classify	inference	omit	system
accumulation	compile	involve	procedure	systematic
acquire	contemplate	latter	proceed	version
analysis	exclude	manner	strategize	

1. an amount that collects __ __ __ __ __ __ __ __ __ __ __ __
                                            1   2

2. a careful study of the parts to understand the whole __ __ __ __ __ __ __ __
                                                                          3

3. to think about seriously __ __ __ __ __ __ __ __ __ __ __
                                      4

4. to suppose or guess __ __ __ __ __ __ __
                                    5

5. an answer found by using facts you learn __ __ __ __ __ __ __ __ __
                                                                6

6. a step-by-step way of doing something __ __ __ __ __ __ __ __ __
                                                            7

7. a way in which something is done __ __ __ __ __ __
                                                  8

8. to use a strategy to plan __ __ __ __ __ __ __ __ __ __
                                    9   10

Now use the numbers under the letters to crack the code. Write the letters on the lines below. The words will complete this sentence:

Because they are so hard, diamonds are used to _____.

__ __ __   h __ __   __ __ __ __ __ __
4 1 8   3 6 7   5 10 8 3 2 9

approximate • approximately
comparable • absolute • absolutely

Use the reproducible definitions on page 176 and the suggestions on page 6 to introduce the words for each day.

DAY 1

approximate
(adj.) More or less accurate or correct. *We only need to report the approximate length of the hallway.*

Say: *Approximate is the opposite of "exact."* Then ask: *What could you do to get the approximate height of someone?* (e.g., use your own height and guess the difference) *When would it be OK to be approximate? Building a piece of furniture? Baking a cake? Reporting the number of days until school is out?* Then have students complete the Day 1 activities on page 83. You may want to do the first one as a group.

DAY 2

approximately
(adv.) Not exactly, but nearly. *We have approximately one hour to work on the project.*

Say: *When a measurement is nearly exact, we use the word approximately to describe it. For example, I am approximately (give an estimation in feet or inches) from my desk.* Ask students to tell **approximately** how much time is left in today's school day, the month, and the year. Then have students complete the Day 2 activities on page 83. You may want to do the first one as a group.

DAY 3

comparable
(adj.) Nearly the same; similar. *Both pairs of sneakers are comparable in price.*

Review what students do when they compare. (See how two things are alike.) Note the difference in pronunciation between "compare" and **comparable**. Say: *When two things are similar, we say they are comparable.* Hold up a regular and a mechanical pencil. Ask: *Are these things comparable? Why?* (both pencils; both used for writing) Then ask: *What kinds of words are comparable?* (synonyms) Then have students complete the Day 3 activities on page 84. You may want to do the first one as a group.

DAY 4

absolute
(adj.) Complete; total; without limit. *I have absolute confidence in my ability to do this activity.*

absolutely
(adv.) Completely; totally. *I checked my work, and I am absolutely sure it is correct.*

Say: *Be absolutely quiet for 10 seconds.* Allow this to happen. Ask: *Were you absolutely silent?* (possibly) *Did we have absolute silence?* (no) *Was there any noise whatsoever?* (e.g., outside noises; other classes; shuffling) *What must have happened to have absolute silence?* (no sounds at all) Then ask: *If someone has absolute power, what does that mean?* (total, complete power) *What kinds of people have absolute power?* (dictators; monarchs) Then have students complete the Day 4 activities on page 84. You may want to do the first one as a group.

DAY 5

Have students complete page 85. Call on students to read aloud their answers to the writing activity.

Name_____

Day 1 approximate

1. **How would you complete this sentence? Say it aloud to a partner.**

   The approximate height of my _____ is _____.

2. **Your parent wants to know the *approximate* cost of a school activity.**
   What does that mean? Circle your answer.

   a. Your parent wants a close amount of how much the activity costs.
   b. Your parent wants to know the exact amount that the activity will cost.
   c. Your parent wants an idea of why you are interested in the activity.
   d. Your parent wants you to earn the money to pay for the activity.

3. **What do you think is the *approximate* number of students present in class today?**

   _____

Day 2 approximately

1. **How would you complete this sentence? Say it aloud to a partner.**

   There are approximately _____ until my birthday.

2. **A family has planned *approximately* five days for a trip. What does that mean?**
   Circle your answer.

   a. The trip must be completed in five days.
   b. The family actually has about three days for a trip.
   c. Some family members will stay home if the trip takes longer than five days.
   d. A family has about five days for a trip but may actually have more or fewer days.

3. **Which sentence does _not_ use *approximately* correctly? Circle your answer.**

   a. The plane will arrive at approximately 8 p.m.
   b. I can give you an approximately number of students.
   c. This tree will take approximately two years to bear fruit.
   d. The school pond is approximately 80 feet wide.

4. ***Approximately* how long does it take you to complete a *Daily Academic Vocabulary* lesson?**

   _____

   _____

Name_____

Day 3   comparable

1. How would you complete this sentence? Say it aloud to a partner.

Two games with comparable rules are _____ and _____.

2. If you and a friend have *comparable* skills in math, which of these is true? Circle your answer.

    a.   Your friend is much better in math than you are.
    b.   You are much better in math than your friend.
    c.   You and your friend have about the same ability in math.
    d.   Your friend always tries to do math problems faster than you.

3. Which of these would <u>not</u> be true of two activities that are *comparable* in difficulty? Circle your answer.

    a.   Both activities require about the same amount of skill.
    b.   One activity is much easier to do than the other.
    c.   One activity is about as challenging as the other.
    d.   Neither activity is more difficult than the other.

Day 4   absolute • absolutely

1. How would you complete these sentences? Say them aloud to a partner.

If I had absolute freedom, I would _____.

I am absolutely against _____ because _____.

2. A teacher asks for your *absolute* attention. What do you need to do? Circle your answer.

    a.   Keep on doing what you are doing.
    b.   Listen with one ear while you finish what you are doing.
    c.   Stop what you are doing and pay full attention to the teacher.
    d.   Stop what you are doing and get ready to leave the classroom.

Give me your **absolute** attention!

3. Which word is <u>not</u> a synonym for *absolutely*? Circle your answer.

    a.   finally   c.   wholly
    b.   entirely   d.   completely

Name_____

Daily Academic Vocabulary

Fill in the bubble next to the correct answer.

1. In which sentence is *approximate* <u>not</u> used correctly?

Ⓐ Monday or Tuesday is the approximate day when the packages will arrive.

Ⓑ The approximate number of days for shipping is three or four.

Ⓒ We need an approximate number of the guests in order to buy food.

Ⓓ We will approximate the party if we know exactly when it begins.

2. Which word is an antonym for *approximately*?

Ⓕ roughly

Ⓖ precisely

Ⓗ around

Ⓙ nearly

3. If two sports are *comparable,* which statement would be used to describe them?

Ⓐ They are nothing alike.

Ⓑ The only thing they have in common is they are played by a team.

Ⓒ One sport requires helmets and the other does not.

Ⓓ Both use similar equipment and are played in much the same way.

4. In which sentence could *absolutely* replace the underlined word?

Ⓕ We will <u>never</u> have enough time to see the movie.

Ⓖ We can <u>maybe</u> have time for a visit to the beach.

Ⓗ We <u>completely</u> failed to send a postcard to anyone.

Ⓙ We <u>almost</u> ran out of water and had only one bottle left.

Writing   Should anyone have *absolute* power over other people? Why or why not?
Be sure to use at least one of this week's words in your writing.

_____

_____

_____

_____

debate • issue

Use the reproducible definitions on page 177 and the suggestions on page 6 to introduce the words for each day.

DAY 1

debate
(verb) To discuss the arguments for or against something. *Our class will debate another class about the choice of school mascot.*

(noun) A discussion of arguments for or against something. *There was a debate between two classes over the choice of school mascot.*

Ask: *How would you debate another class?* (e.g., give arguments back and forth) *Where have you seen or heard of people debating?* (e.g., in history books; on television) Then ask: *What is the difference between arguing and debating?* (e.g., opinion versus facts; argument is often more emotional) *What are some topics we might debate in school?* Then explain that **debate** can also be a noun. Ask: *Have you ever seen or been in a debate? Tell us about it. What did you debate?* Encourage students to use the word **debate** in their responses. Then have students complete the Day 1 activities on page 87. You may want to do the first one as a group.

DAY 2

debate
(verb) To think over carefully before making a decision. *I debated whether to play in the band or sing in the chorus.*

Say: *You can also debate with yourself.* Ask: *What would you do if you were debating between two things?* (e.g., think of pros and cons of both) *Have you ever had to debate about something? What did you do?* Then have students complete the Day 2 activities on page 87. You may want to do the first one as a group.

DAY 3

issue
(noun) A subject of debate or argument. *The classes discussed the issue of student rights.*

Explain that a topic that people debate is called an **issue**. Refer to the sample sentence. Ask: *What are other issues important to students that a class might discuss? What are some common issues you think people debate? What issues would you like to debate?* Encourage students to use vocabulary words in their responses. Then have students complete the Day 3 activities on page 88. You may want to do the first one as a group.

DAY 4

issue
(verb) To send or give out something. *The principal will issue a statement that recognizes students for their participation in the recycling program.*

Point out that **issue** can also be a verb. Say: *Things can be issued in speech or in writing, or even given to someone. For example, a king can issue a proclamation, and a school can issue lockers to students.* Discuss how these examples are **issued**. Then ask: *What is something that students might issue?* (e.g. a publication; a request; an award) Then have students complete the Day 4 activities on page 88. You may want to do the first one as a group.

DAY 5

Have students complete page 89. Call on students to read aloud their answers to the writing activity.

Name_____

Day 1 debate

1. How would you complete these sentences? Say them aloud to a partner.

I would prepare for a debate by _____.

I would like to see a debate between _____ and _____ on the topic of _____.

2. Your teacher invites the class to *debate* the need for homework. What does that mean? Circle your answer.

   a. Your teacher will no longer give homework.
   b. Your class enjoys getting homework.
   c. Your class will present reasons why homework is or is not helpful.
   d. Your teacher will decide if homework is helpful or not for each student.

3. Which of these would <u>not</u> be true of a good *debate* between two classes? Circle your answer.

   a. Neither class would have anything to say.
   b. There would be a discussion between the classes.
   c. Both sides would have different points of view.
   d. Each class would present arguments to challenge the other.

Day 2 debate

1. How would you complete this sentence? Say it aloud to a partner.

Something my family might debate is _____.

2. When it starts to rain, the umpire *debates* stopping the baseball game. Which of these would <u>not</u> be true? Circle your answer.

   a. The umpire considers the safety of both teams.
   b. The umpire immediately stops the game.
   c. The umpire thinks about what happens if the rain continues.
   d. The umpire thinks about what happens if the game is stopped.

3. When you *debate* between two activities, what do you do? Circle your answer.

   a. You find out what your friends are doing.
   b. You choose the first activity you think of.
   c. You flip a coin to decide.
   d. You think about the positives and negatives of each activity.

Daily
Academic
Vocabulary

Day 3 | issue

1. How would you complete this sentence? Say it aloud to a partner.

I think an important issue is _____.

2. Which word would least likely be used to describe an *issue* that people argue about? Circle your answer.

a. unimportant
b. critical
c. political
d. interesting

3. If the *issue* for a family is where to go on vacation, what does that mean? Circle your answer.

a. Everyone in the family agrees on where to go for a vacation.
b. No one in the family wants to take a vacation.
c. The family is discussing where to go on vacation.
d. The family is on vacation and doesn't want to leave.

Day 4 | issue

1. How would you complete this sentence? Say it aloud to a partner.

A weather expert might issue a warning about _____.

2. Players *issue* a challenge to another team. What does that mean? Circle your answer.

a. The players are fighting on the field.
b. The players send a challenge to another team.
c. The players produce a magazine for the other team.
d. The players are afraid of a challenge.

I **issue** a challenge to anyone who thinks parrots are ugly.

3. When schools *issue* a schedule for the year, what do they do? Circle your answer.

a. They give out a schedule for when school is in session.
b. They keep the schedule a secret.
c. They look for someone to create a schedule.
d. They argue about which days students will be in school.

Day 5 debate • issue

Fill in the bubble next to the correct answer.

1. Which of these would <u>not</u> be required to *debate* someone?

Ⓐ a topic to discuss

Ⓑ a strong opinion

Ⓒ speaking or writing your ideas

Ⓓ a very loud voice

2. In which sentence could *debate* fill in the blank?

Ⓕ My science report will include a _____ and a summary.

Ⓖ There is often a _____ among scientists over a theory.

Ⓗ The science experiment needs a _____ to be complete.

Ⓙ We can find a _____ to display for the science fair.

3. In which sentence could *debate* replace the underlined word?

Ⓐ We need to <u>arrange</u> a time to meet for the movie.

Ⓑ I have chores to <u>complete</u> before the movie.

Ⓒ I need to <u>consider</u> whether to ride the bus or walk.

Ⓓ We need to <u>discover</u> a new way to get around.

4. Which pair of words are both synonyms for *issue*?

Ⓕ subject—send

Ⓖ factor—translate

Ⓗ idea—attempt

Ⓙ process—include

Writing   Describe an *issue* that friends may argue about and explain how to deal with it. Be sure to use at least one of this week's words in your writing.

_____

_____

_____

_____

concise • compact • condensed
condense • cohesive

Use the reproducible definitions on page 178 and the suggestions on page 6 to introduce the words for each day.

DAY 1

concise
(adj.) Saying a lot in a few words. *A dictionary gives a concise definition of each word.*

Say: *See if you can name the story from this concise summary.* Summarize a familiar tale such as "Cinderella" in two or three sentences. Then talk about situations in which students generally need to be **concise**. (e.g., giving instructions; poetry; expository writing) Then have students complete the Day 1 activities on page 91. You may want to do the first one as a group.

DAY 2

compact
(adj.) Not taking up too much space. *We have small lockers so our belongings have to be compact.*

Say: *When something is compact, it is usually made small enough so that it can fit into tight spaces.* Show students two books, such as a large textbook and a small paperback. Ask: *Which book is more compact?* (the paperback) *Why do you think this book was made to be compact?* (carry it around easily) Then ask: *What other things can you think of that are compact?* (e.g., **compact** cars; small music players; cellphones) Then have students complete the Day 2 activities on page 91. You may want to do the first one as a group.

DAY 3

condensed
(adj.) Shortened or made smaller. *A condensed story has the less important parts cut out.*

condense
(verb) To make smaller or shorter. *You must condense the report to fit on only one page.*

Ask: *Have you ever heard of a condensed version of a book?* Explain what it is and discuss what a **condensed** book may not include. (e.g., some characters and events) Then ask: *What other things might need to be condensed?* (e.g., speeches; recess; school day) Discuss how to **condense** a speech. How would students make the speech shorter? Have students practice by **condensing** the sample sentence or other sentences you give them. (e.g., **Condense** the report to one page.) Then have students complete the Day 3 activities on page 92. You may want to do the first one as a group.

DAY 4

cohesive
(adj.) Holding or working together as a whole. *A cohesive team cooperates to get a job done.*

Have students describe how a team acts when it is **cohesive**. (e.g., sticks together; shares ideas; has one goal) Then ask: *How could a group working on a project be cohesive? Why is it important for the group to be cohesive?* Then have students complete the Day 4 activities on page 92. You may want to do the first one as a group.

DAY 5

Have students complete page 93. Call on students to read aloud their answers to the writing activity.

Daily Academic Vocabulary • EMC 2762 • © Evan-Moor Corp.

Name_____

Day 1 concise

1. How would you complete this sentence? Say it aloud to a partner.

If asked to give a concise description of our classroom, I would say _____.

2. If your teacher asks for a clear and *concise* answer, what should you do?
Circle your answer.

    a. Answer in the form of a short report.

    b. Answer very quickly.

    c. Describe the entire process you followed to get the answer.

    d. Give an answer that is brief and to the point.

3. Which phrase would describe a *concise* explanation? Circle your answer.

    a. careless and foolish   c. short and direct

    b. twisting and turning   d. long and boring

4. Give a *concise* answer to this question:
What do you learn by studying academic vocabulary?

_____

_____

_____

Day 2 compact

1. How would you complete this sentence? Say it aloud to a partner.

Something compact that I own is _____.

2. Which word is an antonym for *compact*? Circle your answer.

    a. enormous   c. slender

    b. miniature   d. reduced

3. Which of these would <u>not</u> be true of a *compact* car? Circle your answer.

    a. It has two doors.   c. It can carry a few people.

    b. It is very long and wide.   d. It can fit in small parking spaces.

Daily Academic Vocabulary

Day 3 condensed • condense

1. How would you complete these sentences? Say them aloud to a partner.

_____ can be condensed.

I would condense _____ by _____.

2. If you had a *condensed* week of school, what would that mean? Circle your answer.

    a. You would have a tough week at school.

    b. Your class would shrink in size.

    c. There would be fewer days of school than normal.

    d. There would be fewer students at school than normal.

3. Which sentence uses *condense* corrrectly? Circle your answer.

    a. If we condense the map, it will be larger and easier to read.

    b. Everything is wet because of the condense outside.

    c. My friends and I can condense for a short time.

    d. We could condense our trip if we eliminate a few stops.

How can I condense this book?

BIG BIRD BOOK

Day 4 cohesive

1. How would you complete this sentence? Say it aloud to a partner.

A cohesive family would _____.

2. Which word is a synonym for *cohesive*? Circle your answer.

    a. disorganized   c. disloyal

    b. united   d. precise

3. Which of these does <u>not</u> describe a *cohesive* plan of action? Circle your answer.

    a. It does not make any sense.

    b. It is clear how the steps lead to a final product.

    c. Each step of the plan leads to the next step.

    d. It holds together and shows good thinking.

4. How would you describe a *cohesive* piece of writing?

_____

_____

Name_____

Fill in the bubble next to the correct answer.

1. In which sentence is *concise* used correctly?

Ⓐ Her letters are concise and filled with news about people we don't even know.

Ⓑ The concise man was big and tall, just like the tall tales he liked to tell.

Ⓒ We need concise directions so we are not confused by too much information.

Ⓓ The concise description of the house included every little detail.

2. In which sentence is *compact* <u>not</u> used correctly?

Ⓕ The backpack is compact and easy to carry.

Ⓖ Bunk beds are compact and good for a small room.

Ⓗ A compact computer can fit in almost any work area.

Ⓘ A compact notebook is larger than the usual kind.

3. In which sentence could *condensed* replace the underlined word?

Ⓐ This activity is <u>shorter</u> and takes less time than the original.

Ⓑ There is a <u>larger</u> part of the puzzle to finish.

Ⓒ There is a <u>surprise</u> ending to that story.

Ⓓ This photograph is <u>brighter</u> than the others.

4. In which sentence could *condense* fill in the blank?

Ⓕ The movie had to _____ new characters to make the story more interesting.

Ⓖ The poem is long, but we will ruin the rhyming pattern if we _____ it.

Ⓗ The play is better when we _____ characters that are not needed.

Ⓘ The novel is about the main character trying to _____ his family.

Writing   Describe your idea of a *cohesive* group of friends. Be sure to use
the word *cohesive* in your writing.

_____

_____

_____

_____

insert • insertion
delete • deletion

Use the reproducible definitions on page 179 and the suggestions on page 6 to introduce the words for each day.

DAY 1

insert
(verb) To put, or place inside something. *You should insert a comma between the city and state.*

insertion
(noun) The act of inserting. *The insertion of a comma will correct the error.*

Say: *When you put one thing in something else, you insert it.* Ask: *How do you use the word insert at school?* (e.g., **insert** a word or a sentence; in science experiments) *How do you use the word at home?* (e.g., **insert** filling between slices of bread to make a sandwich; insert tab A into slot B) Then say: *When you insert, you make an insertion.* Show a stack of books. **Insert** a book into the middle of the stack. Ask: *What did I just make?* (an **insertion**) Then have students complete the Day 1 activities on page 95. You may want to do the first one as a group.

DAY 2

insertion
(noun) Something, such as a word or phrase, that has been inserted. *A comma was the only insertion that was needed in your entire report.*

Say: *Insertion is also the thing that is inserted.* Show a stack of books again. Insert a book into the middle of the stack. Ask: *What did I just make?* (an insertion) *What was the insertion?* (the book) Then compare and contrast the sample sentences from Days 1 and 2 to help students distinguish between the two meanings. Have students complete the Day 2 activities on page 95. You may want to do the first one as a group.

DAY 3

delete
(verb) To remove from a piece of writing or computer text. *Please delete the period and add a question mark.*

deletion
(noun) The act of deleting. *The deletion of a period takes one touch of a computer key.*

Ask: *How do you delete something from your writing?* (e.g., cross it out; press the delete key on the keyboard) Point out that **delete** is the opposite of "insert" from Day 1. Then say: *You make a deletion when you delete something.* Discuss the meaning and confirm that it is the opposite of "insertion" from Day 1. Demonstrate **delete** and **deletion** by using your word processing program if you have a smart board or large screen for your computer. Then have students complete the Day 3 activities on page 96. You may want to do the first one as a group.

DAY 4

deletion
(noun) Something, such as a word or phrase, that has been deleted. *You made the wrong deletion and now the sentence doesn't make sense.*

Say: *What you delete is also called a deletion.* Point out that this definition of **deletion** is the opposite of "insertion" from Day 2. Ask: *If I type the sentence "I like small dogs" and then delete the word "small," what is the deletion?* ("small") Then have students complete the Day 4 activities on page 96. You may want to do the first one as a group.

DAY 5

Have students complete page 97. Call on students to read aloud their answers to the writing activity.

Name_____

Day 1 insert • insertion

1. How would you complete these sentences? Say them aloud to a partner.

I would like to insert _____ into my usual day.

The insertion of more books on the classroom shelves would _____.

2. During a science experiment, you *insert* a straw into a bottle. What do you do? Circle your answer.

   a. Use the straw to drink.

   b. Place the straw next to the bottle.

   c. Put the straw inside the bottle.

   d. Measure the straw and the bottle.

3. Which sentence uses *insertion* correctly? Circle your answer.

   a. The insertion of an extra hour makes our school day longer.

   b. More students would take part in an art class insertion.

   c. The coaches plan to insertion a new sport this year.

   d. The student has an insertion of the rules to explain.

Day 2 insertion

1. How would you complete this sentence? Say it aloud to a partner.

When I check my writing, I often have to make an insertion of _____.

2. An *insertion* is needed to correct a misspelled word. What does that mean? Circle your answer.

   a. You have used the wrong letter.

   b. You need to add the missing letter.

   c. You need to write a new sentence.

   d. A sentence is missing many important words.

3. Which of these would <u>never</u> be true of a sentence after an *insertion* was added? Circle your answer.

   a. The sentence would be clearer.

   b. The sentence would be longer.

   c. The sentence would be more interesting.

   d. The sentence would be shorter.

Name _____

Day 3 | delete • deletion

1. **How would you complete these sentences? Say them aloud to a partner.**

   I would like to delete _____ from my usual week.

   I think the deletion of _____ from _____ would be a good idea.

2. **The cafeteria has to *delete* items from the lunch menu. What does that mean? Circle your answer.**

   a. There will be fewer items on the menu.
   b. There will be more items on the menu.
   c. The menu will not change.
   d. The cafeteria will stop serving lunch.

3. **The *deletion* of a rule would have what result? Circle your answer.**

   a. The wording of the rule would change.
   b. The rule would no longer have to be followed.
   c. The rule would be easier to understand.
   d. The rule would only be used now and then.

Day 4 | deletion

1. **How would you complete this sentence? Say it aloud to a partner.**

   The deletion of _____ would make a paragraph hard to read.

2. **Which word is an antonym for *deletion*? Circle your answer.**

   a. improvement   c. illustration
   b. direction   d. addition

3. **Which sentence uses *deletion* correctly? Circle your answer.**

   a. The deletion made the sentence too wordy.
   b. One more deletion will add just the right word.
   c. This deletion made the sentence more concise.
   d. A sentence that needs a deletion is usually too clear.

4. **Rewrite this sentence, but with a *deletion*:**
   If at first you don't succeed, try, try again.

Parrots are ~~not~~ the smartest birds.

_____

_____

Name_____

Daily
Academic
Vocabulary

Day 5 insert • insertion • delete • deletion

Fill in the bubble next to the correct answer.

1. Which of these would <u>not</u> be an example of an *insertion*?

    Ⓐ a word in a sentence

    Ⓑ a sentence in a paragraph

    Ⓒ a paragraph in an essay

    Ⓓ a title of a story

2. In which sentence does *insertion* mean "the act of inserting"?

    Ⓕ The insertion of a heavy object caused the tub of water to overflow.

    Ⓖ That block in the middle was the insertion that made the tower stronger.

    Ⓗ That phrase was a great insertion to add to our conclusion.

    Ⓙ Adding his opinion was the wrong insertion when facts were needed.

3. When you delete something, what happens to the *deletion*?

    Ⓐ It is added.

    Ⓑ It is gone.

    Ⓒ It is revised.

    Ⓓ It is not changed.

4. In which sentence could *deletion* fill in the blank?

    Ⓕ The _____ of the cooking class means no more cooking lessons.

    Ⓖ The _____ of our team means we will get to play ball this year.

    Ⓗ The _____ of that mystery will continue for a long time.

    Ⓙ The _____ of a new planet would be an exciting adventure.

Writing   Describe a rule that you would *insert* into a set of rules for your team, class, or school. Use the word *insert* or *insertion* in your writing.

_____

_____

_____

_____

WEEK 23

foresee • anticipate
anticipation • expectation

Use the reproducible definitions on page 180 and the suggestions on page 6 to introduce the words for each day.

DAY 1

foresee
(verb) To see or realize in advance that something will happen. *The teacher could* **foresee** *that the students who followed the directions carefully would produce a better project.*

Have students identify the word parts. ("fore-" and "see") Explain the meaning of "fore-" (before; earlier) applied to "see." Confirm by giving the definition. Ask: *What could enable a person to* **foresee** *an outcome or event?* (e.g., using evidence or previous experience) Ask: *What do you* **foresee** *happening next in class?* (e.g., doing the word activities) Then have students complete the Day 1 activities on page 99. You may want to do the first one as a group.

DAY 2

anticipate
(verb) To expect. *The students* **anticipate** *the usual Friday quiz.*

anticipation
(noun) The act or process of anticipating. *In* **anticipation** *of the Friday quiz, most students reviewed their notes on Thursday.*

Say: *I* **anticipate** *that I will ___ after school.* Ask: *When you* **anticipate**, *what do you do?* (expect) *What do you* **anticipate** *will happen tomorrow?* Then say: *When you are* **anticipating** *something, you are in* **anticipation** *of it.* Ask: *What do you do on Friday in* **anticipation** *of a weekend?* (e.g., make plans) Encourage students to use the words **anticipate** and **anticipation** in their responses. Then have students complete the Day 2 activities on page 99. You may want to do the first one as a group.

DAY 3

expectation
(noun) The feeling or belief that something is likely to happen. *It is our* **expectation** *that we will have fun on the field trip.*

Ask: *What does it mean when you "expect" something?* (you think something will happen) Guide students to use this knowledge to understand the meaning of **expectation**. Point out that an **expectation** often develops from experience or knowledge. Ask: *What are your* **expectations** *for the rest of the day?* (e.g., usual schedule) *What are your* **expectations** *for the next school year?* Then have students complete the Day 3 activities on page 100. You may want to do the first one as a group.

DAY 4

expectation
(noun) A standard of conduct or performance expected. *The student lived up to the* **expectations** *of her teacher by passing the test.*

Say: *My* **expectations** *of you are very high.* Ask: *What specific* **expectations** *do I have of you?* (e.g., to work hard; to behave) Then have students give their **expectations** of an upcoming school event, such as a concert or assembly. Have students complete the Day 4 activities on page 100. You may want to do the first one as a group.

DAY 5

Have students complete page 101. Call on students to read aloud their answers to the writing activity.

Name_____

Day 1 foresee

1. How would you complete this sentence? Say it aloud to a partner.

I can foresee that I will _____ if I _____.

2. A baseball heads for a window and you *foresee* the window breaking. What does that mean? Circle your answer.

   a. You plan to break the window.

   b. You know the window will break before it happens.

   c. You wish the window would break.

   d. You saw a broken window and guessed what happened.

3. The music teacher says she can *foresee* a career for you as a singer. What does that mean? Circle your answer.

   a. She has excellent sight.

   b. She believes in working hard to be a good singer.

   c. She likes to listen to you sing.

   d. She believes you could work as a singer someday.

Day 2 anticipate • anticipation

1. How would you complete these sentences? Say them aloud to a partner.

I anticipate that I will _____ this year because _____.

In my family, the anticipation before _____ is always exciting because _____.

2. If you *anticipate* that you will get a high score on a test, which of these is <u>not</u> true? Circle your answer.

   a. You expect to do well on the test.

   b. You will be surprised if you get a bad grade.

   c. You will be shocked if you get a good grade.

   d. You knew the information on the test.

3. The *anticipation* of a game makes the team nervous. What does that mean? Circle your answer.

   a. The game was played and the team lost.

   b. The team is nervous from thinking about the game.

   c. The team is nervous because no one knows where the game will be played.

   d. No one expects the team to win.

Daily Academic Vocabulary

Day 3 | **expectation**

1. How would you complete this sentence? Say it aloud to a partner.

An expectation I have for next week is that _____ will happen because _____.

2. People have the *expectation* that the storm could cause a flood. What does that mean? Circle your answer.

　　a.　People are hoping for rain.
　　b.　People are predicting a flood could occur.
　　c.　People have just learned that storms cause floods.
　　d.　People talk too much about the weather.

3. If your *expectation* is that science classes will be more difficult in college, then which of these is true? Circle your answer.

　　a.　You believe that science classes will be harder in college.
　　b.　You hope that science class is more work in college.
　　c.　You know that science classes will be easier in college.
　　d.　You think science is fun to learn.

Day 4 | **expectation**

1. How would you complete this sentence? Say it aloud to a partner.

I hope to live up to the expectations of _____.

2. Which of these is least likely to be your *expectation* of a movie with your favorite star? Circle your answer.

　　a.　You think it will be fun to see the movie.
　　b.　You think you will enjoy the movie.
　　c.　You think the star will do a good job.
　　d.　You think the movie will be terrible.

3. The coach's *expectation* of the team is high. What does that mean? Circle your answer.

　　a.　The coach is looking up at the team.
　　b.　The coach has a team of tall players.
　　c.　The coach expects the team to do well.
　　d.　The coach wonders if the team can win.

4. What is an *expectation* you have of your friends?

Name _____

Day 5 | foresee • anticipate
anticipation • expectation

Fill in the bubble next to the correct answer.

1. What can you do if you are able to *foresee* a problem?

Ⓐ Solve the problem after it occurs.

Ⓑ Let the problem get bigger.

Ⓒ Avoid the problem before it occurs.

Ⓓ Make a mistake.

2. Which word or phrase is a synonym for *anticipate*?

Ⓕ expect

Ⓖ move ahead

Ⓗ give up

Ⓙ give back

3. In which sentence could *anticipation* fill in the blank?

Ⓐ My _____ was not fun because it rained.

Ⓑ I look forward to summer with happy _____.

Ⓒ The _____ was noisy because of so many people.

Ⓓ We plan to have lots of _____ this summer.

4. Which word is <u>not</u> a synonym for *expectation*?

Ⓕ belief

Ⓖ prediction

Ⓗ assumption

Ⓙ accomplishment

I have high-flying **expectations** of myself!

Writing Who has *expectations* for you? What are they? Do you think you will fulfill those *expectations*? Use at least one of this week's words in your writing.

_____

_____

_____

_____

_____

subsequent • precede preceding • prior

Use the reproducible definitions on page 181 and the suggestions on page 6 to introduce the words for each day.

DAY 1

subsequent
(adj.) Coming after in time or order. *If we lose this round, we will need to win the subsequent round to stay in the tournament.*

Say: *Let's pretend that we are reading a fiction book and discussing why a character acted in a particular way. If I said to you, "In subsequent chapters, you will discover the reasons for the character's actions," what would that mean?* (in the chapters that follow) Then ask: *If I asked you to skim a chapter in your social studies book to find the subsequent results of a specific event, what would you do?* (look for events that came after the event named) Then have students complete the Day 1 activities on page 103. You may want to do the first one as a group.

DAY 2

precede
(verb) To come before in time. *For many children, a year of preschool precedes kindergarten.*

Ask: *What months precede this month in the year? What things do you do that precede your arrival at school?* (e.g., getting ready; eating breakfast) *What are movies often preceded by?* (previews or ads) Encourage students to use the word **precede** in their responses. Then have students complete the Day 2 activities on page 103. You may want to do the first one as a group.

DAY 3

preceding
(adj.) Coming just before. *The sky grew very dark in the moments preceding the storm.*

Ask students to turn to page 20 in one of their textbooks. Ask: *What is the preceding page?* (page 19) Ask: *Preceding this class, what did you do?* Then remind students of a story or book you are currently reading in class. Ask: *What happened in the preceding pages of the story?* (students should respond with action that happened immediately before the current actions) Then have students complete the Day 3 activities on page 104. You may want to do the first one as a group.

DAY 4

prior
(adj.) Earlier in time or coming before. *We build on prior knowledge to learn something new.*

Ask: *How would prior knowledge of a genre, such as fiction, help you read a new fiction story? What would you know about it?* (e.g., it wasn't true) Then ask: *What is a favorite story you have read prior to this school year? Who are some of your prior teachers? What grades come prior to sixth grade?* (kindergarten through fifth grade) Then have students complete the Day 4 activities on page 104. You may want to do the first one as a group.

DAY 5

Have students complete page 105. Call on students to read aloud their answers to the writing activity.

Name_____

Day 1 | subsequent

1. How would you complete this sentence? Say it aloud to a partner.

In subsequent years, I expect to _____.

2. Your teacher announces that *subsequent* classes will be held in the library. What does that mean? Circle your answer.

    a. Small classes will meet in the library.

    b. Classes with a substitute teacher will go to the library.

    c. The next classes will be held in the library.

    d. The lower grades are using the library.

3. Your introductory paragraph to an essay is strong, but the *subsequent* paragraphs need work. What should you do? Circle your answer.

    a. Revise your introductory paragraph.

    b. Focus on improving the paragraphs after the introduction.

    c. Rewrite your entire essay.

    d. Focus on improving your concluding paragraph.

Day 2 | precede

1. How would you complete this sentence? Say it aloud to a partner.

_____ precedes _____ in my school schedule.

2. If a pizza party will *precede* a movie, which of these is true? Circle your answer.

    a. Most kids will be hungry during the movie.

    b. The party will take place after the movie.

    c. Kids will have pizza during the movie.

    d. Kids will have pizza before the movie.

3. A talk with an artist will *precede* a class tour of the art museum. What does that mean? Circle your answer.

    a. The first activity at the museum is meeting the artist.

    b. The second activity at the museum is meeting the artist.

    c. The tour will take place first.

    d. The artist will talk during the tour.

Lightning **precedes** thunder in a storm!

Name _____

Daily Academic Vocabulary

Day 3 **preceding**

1. How would you complete this sentence? Say it aloud to a partner.

In the days preceding an important test, I _____.

2. Which of these is true of a bell *preceding* a fire drill? Circle your answer.

   a. The bell signals that a fire drill will follow.

   b. The bell rings several hours before the fire drill.

   c. The bell signals that the fire drill is over.

   d. There is no warning before the fire drill.

3. Which of these is always true of a *preceding* event? Circle your answer.

   a. It is too long.   c. It comes before something else.

   b. It is too short.   d. It comes after something else.

Day 4 **prior**

1. How would you complete this sentence? Say it aloud to a partner.

A sport or other activity I did prior to this year is _____.

2. If you have *prior* plans, why will you miss the game at school? Circle your answer.

   a. You don't know who planned the game.

   b. You don't know where the game is.

   c. You would rather see your friends after the game.

   d. You have other plans that you made earlier.

3. Which of these describes a *prior* solution? Circle your answer.

   a. one that was just discovered

   b. one that was discovered earlier

   c. one that has not been discovered

   d. one that does not work

4. What did you do *prior* to working on *Daily Academic Vocabulary*?

_____

_____

_____

Name_____

Daily Academic Vocabulary

Day 5 **subsequent • precede • preceding • prior**

Fill in the bubble next to the correct answer.

1. In which sentence is *subsequent* used correctly?

Ⓐ The subsequent information always comes first.

Ⓑ There is a subsequent to plan.

Ⓒ We can subsequent for the team that is late.

Ⓓ Each subsequent grade in school is more challenging.

2. Which word is an antonym for *precede*?

Ⓕ guide

Ⓖ follow

Ⓗ finish

Ⓙ lead

3. If the *preceding* day was a great one for you, which sentence is true?

Ⓐ Yesterday was a great day for you.

Ⓑ Last week had several great days.

Ⓒ Tomorrow will be a great day.

Ⓓ Today is a great day.

4. If you use *prior* knowledge to answer a question, which of these is true?

Ⓕ You use something you just learned to answer the question.

Ⓖ You answer the question in complete sentences.

Ⓗ You use something you already knew to answer the question.

Ⓙ You answer this question before another one.

Writing   Describe a *prior* experience that has helped you this year. Be sure to use the word *prior* in your writing.

_____

_____

_____

_____

distinguish • discriminate distinction

Use the reproducible definitions on page 182 and the suggestions on page 6 to introduce the words for each day.

DAY 1

distinguish
(verb) To tell apart by knowing or seeing the difference between two things. *We distinguish between the two students by the color of their hair.*

Display two classroom objects, such as a stapler and a marker. Ask: *What can you see to help distinguish between these items?* (e.g., size; shape) *What things do you know that help distinguish between them?* (e.g., their uses) Then ask: *How can you distinguish among books?* Students should respond with things they can see and things they know. Then have students complete the Day 1 activities on page 107. You may want to do the first one as a group.

DAY 2

distinguish
(verb) To see or hear clearly. *I could not distinguish her voice on the phone because she was whispering.*

Ask: *If you can distinguish a friend's face in a crowd, what can you do?* (e.g., see your friend's face) Then ask students to complete the following sentence: "It was very foggy and the buildings across the river were hard to ___." Ask: *Could you clearly see the buildings?* (No) *So, what could you not do?* (distinguish the buildings) Then have students complete the Day 2 activities on page 107. You may want to do the first one as a group.

DAY 3

discriminate
(verb) To see a clear difference between things, people, or behavior. *A chef can discriminate between the flavors in foods.*

Say: *You probably know that discriminate means "to treat someone unfairly." This definition simply means "to see a clear difference."* Ask students to imagine a dish of salt and a dish of sugar, or demonstrate with the real items. Ask: *Can you use color to discriminate between salt and sugar?* (no) *What would you use to discriminate between them?* (taste) Then have students complete the Day 3 activities on page 108. You may want to do the first one as a group.

DAY 4

distinction
(noun) A feature that makes someone or something different. *Even though they are twins, there are definite distinctions in their personalities.*

Ask: *What is the distinction between salt and sugar?* (different tastes) Say: *The distinction in taste makes those two things different.* Ask: *What qualities give individuals their distinctions?* (e.g., traits; achievements; personalities) Point out that **distinction** usually refers to something that stands out. Then ask: *What is one distinction of our class? What makes us different?* Encourage students to use the word **distinction** in their responses. Then have students complete the Day 4 activities on page 108. You may want to do the first one as a group.

DAY 5

Have students complete page 109. Call on students to read aloud their answers to the writing activity.

Day 1 distinguish

1. How would you complete this sentence? Say it aloud to a partner.

Two animals that are easy to distinguish between are _____ and _____.

2. Which of these would <u>not</u> help you to *distinguish* between two sounds? Circle your answer.

   a. good eyesight
   b. good hearing
   c. knowing what each sound is like
   d. knowing what is different about the sounds

3. If you can *distinguish* between two red flowers, which of these is true? Circle your answer.

   a. The two flowers look exactly alike.
   b. They have qualities that make them different.
   c. Their color is the only important quality you know.
   d. You cannot recognize either kind of flower.

4. What *distinguishes* you from your favorite actor?

_____

_____

Day 2 distinguish

1. How would you complete this sentence? Say it aloud to a partner.

Even from far away, I can usually distinguish _____ because _____.

2. A foggy day makes it hard to *distinguish* many things. What does that mean? Circle your answer.

   a. You cannot smell anything.
   b. You cannot see well.
   c. You cannot think clearly.
   d. You do not feel well.

3. You are waiting in line at a store when you *distinguish* the voice of a friend. What does that mean? Circle your answer.

   a. You are thinking about shopping.
   b. You are thinking about your friend, who has an unusual voice.
   c. You hear the voice of your friend, who is also at the store.
   d. You are bored and wish you had a friend with you.

Day 3 **discriminate**

1. How would you complete this sentence? Say it aloud to a partner.

When people discriminate between soccer and football, they usually think about _____.

2. To *discriminate* one character from another in a story, what must you do? Circle your answer.

 a. Figure out how the characters are alike.

 b. Decide which character you like best.

 c. Explain what is wrong with the characters.

 d. Figure out how the characters are different.

3. You cannot *discriminate* the difference between two pairs of jeans. What does that mean? Circle your answer.

 a. You like one pair of jeans better than the other.

 b. You think the jeans are basically alike.

 c. You know that one pair of jeans belongs to you.

 d. You do not know if the jeans are your size.

Day 4 **distinction**

1. How would you complete this sentence? Say it aloud to a partner.

A distinction between me and my best friend is _____.

2. How would you decide what gives an animal its *distinction*? Circle your answer.

 a. look for qualities that make it friendly

 b. look for qualities that people like

 c. look for qualities that make it special

 d. look for qualities that make it ordinary

3. Which sentence uses *distinction* correctly? Circle your answer.

 a. Their distinction is that they act just alike.

 b. Some people think an asteroid caused the distinction of dinosaurs.

 c. One distinction between children and adults is size.

 d. The teacher was unable to distinction between the twins.

4. What is your primary *distinction*? What makes you different from others?

_____

Name_____

Day 5 distinguish • discriminate • distinction

Fill in the bubble next to the correct answer.

1. If you cannot *distinguish* between twins named Mary and Carrie, which of these is true?

Ⓐ Mary and Carrie look different.

Ⓑ You always know when you see Mary.

Ⓒ You always recognize Carrie.

Ⓓ You cannot tell Mary from Carrie.

2. In which sentence could *distinguish* fill in the blank?

Ⓕ There is a fire that we need to _____.

Ⓖ We could _____ our house in the aerial photograph.

Ⓗ He will _____ how to take good photographs of the children.

Ⓙ I hope we can _____ some fun today.

3. In which sentence is *discriminate* used correctly?

Ⓐ We need to discriminate a plan.

Ⓑ If we discriminate, we should get there on time.

Ⓒ We can always see better when we discriminate.

Ⓓ We can discriminate between good and bad manners.

4. Which adjective would express the meaning of *distinction*?

Ⓕ difference

Ⓖ funny

Ⓗ average

Ⓙ general

*Can you **distinguish** an Amazon parrot from an African Gray parrot?*

Writing   Describe a *distinction* that you like about your school or community. Be sure to use the word *distinction* in your writing.

_____

_____

_____

_____

WEEK 26

construct • constructive
formulate • initiate • initial

Use the reproducible definitions on page 183 and the suggestions on page 6 to introduce the words for each day.

DAY 1

construct
(verb) To build or put together. *We constructed a model of the solar system from styrofoam and hangers.*

Ask: *What things have you constructed?* (e.g., science projects; model planes; treehouses) Point out the connection to the word "construction," which students should know. Ask students to identify both physical and mental things that can be constructed. (e.g., buildings; projects; plans; ideas) Then have students complete the Day 1 activities on page 111. You may want to do the first one as a group.

DAY 2

constructive
(adj.) Serving a useful purpose; helpful. *His constructive comment helped me find a solution to my problem.*

Ask: *If you are trying to solve a problem and someone makes a constructive suggestion, what do they do?* (offer helpful advice) Then ask: *If I have my foot stuck between a chair and a desk, what could you say to me that would be constructive?* Encourage students to respond by completing the sentence, "My constructive suggestion is to ___." (e.g., move the chair; slip your foot out of the shoe) Then have students complete the Day 2 activities on page 111. You may want to do the first one as a group.

DAY 3

formulate
(verb) To work out an idea or opinion or to state something carefully and precisely. *We will formulate a persuasive plan to get permission for a field trip.*

Ask: *Why do you use formulas in math?* (to work out problems or find solutions) Say: *When you work out something or explain an idea carefully, you formulate. We often use this word when we talk about formulating a plan.* Then ask: *How would you formulate a plan to convince your parents to raise your allowance?* Have students complete the Day 3 activities on page 112. You may want to do the first one as a group.

DAY 4

initiate
(verb) To start; to cause to begin. *The warring countries will initiate peace talks.*

initial
(adj.) First, or at the beginning. *Our initial plan was to see a movie, but we went hiking instead.*

Say: *I initiated our lesson by introducing the word initiate. That is how I started the lesson.* Then ask: *How would you initiate a friendship?* (e.g., introduce yourself to someone new) *How would you initiate a meeting on a group project?* Then say: *Initial implies that something follows, like initials in a name. It is something that is first or the beginning.* Ask: *What is the initial stage of the writing process? Describe the initial part of your day.* Then have students complete the Day 4 activities on page 112. You may want to do the first one as a group.

DAY 5

Have students complete page 113. Call on students to read aloud their answers to the writing activity.

Daily
Academic
Vocabulary

Day 1 construct

1. How would you complete this sentence? Say it aloud to a partner.

To construct a _____, I need _____.

2. Your teacher asks you to *construct* a sentence. What do you need to do? Circle your answer.

    a. Find a correct sentence.

    b. Identify what is wrong with a sentence.

    c. Use blocks with letters to build some words.

    d. Put words together to form a sentence.

3. Your assignment is to *construct* a piece of artwork. Which product would <u>not</u> fit the assignment? Circle your answer.

    a. an object you build with pieces of wood

    b. a picture you make by gluing together scraps of paper

    c. a picture of a painting that you cut out from a magazine

    d. an object you form by gluing together tubes of cardboard

Day 2 constructive

1. How would you complete this sentence? Say it aloud to a partner.

When solving a math problem, a constructive tool is _____.

2. Which word is an antonym for *constructive*? Circle your answer.

    a. purposeful   c. positive

    b. destructive   d. promising

3. If a friend offers you *constructive* ideas to solve a problem, which of these is most likely to be true? Circle your answer.

    a. Your friend's ideas will help you build something.

    b. Your friend's ideas are not helpful.

    c. Your friend's ideas may help you solve your problem.

    d. Your friend's ideas will cause a problem you have to solve.

4. If a friend is having a difficult time with an assignment, what might you do that would be *constructive*?

_____

_____

Daily Academic Vocabulary

Day 3 formulate

1. **How would you complete this sentence? Say it aloud to a partner.**

   I should formulate a plan to _____.

2. **Your science teacher challenges you to *formulate* a new invention. What do you need to do? Circle your answer.**

   a. Create a math formula for an invention.

   b. Test a new invention.

   c. Do a report on a new invention you have heard about.

   d. Develop a plan for a new invention.

3. **Which word does <u>not</u> describe how to work when you *formulate* something? Circle your answer.**

   a. slowly   c. precisely

   b. carelessly   d. thoroughly

Day 4 initiate • initial

1. **How would you complete these sentences? Say them aloud to a partner.**

   I wish my teacher would initiate _____.

   My initial impression of our class was _____.

2. **The librarian plans to *initiate* a reading contest. What does that mean? Circle your answer.**

   a. The librarian will start a reading contest.

   b. The librarian will conclude a reading contest.

   c. The librarian will judge a reading contest.

   d. The librarian will stop a reading contest.

3. **If your *initial* answer on a test was wrong, which of these would be true? Circle your answer.**

   a. You answered correctly the first time.

   b. You did not answer the question.

   c. You tried to change your second answer.

   d. You started with the wrong answer.

4. **What were your *initial* thoughts of *Daily Academic Vocabulary?* How have they changed?**

   _____

   _____

Name_____

Day 5 | construct • constructive
formulate • initiate • initial

Fill in the bubble next to the correct answer.

1. In which sentence could *construct* replace the underlined word or words?

Ⓐ The community will <u>tear down</u> the old school.

Ⓑ The children will <u>decorate</u> their bedroom.

Ⓒ The family will <u>build</u> a doghouse in the yard.

Ⓓ The sanitation department will <u>place</u> a trash can on the corner.

2. In which sentence is *formulate* used correctly?

Ⓕ We learned that formulate last year.

Ⓖ It will take time to formulate an entry for the writing contest.

Ⓗ The formulate for winning a contest is to read the rules carefully.

Ⓙ All we need to formulate is a hammer and some nails.

3. In which sentence is *initiate* <u>not</u> used correctly?

Ⓐ Let's initiate the project today so we can finish tomorrow.

Ⓑ Let's initiate the project that was finished yesterday.

Ⓒ We can initiate the project when we get the materials.

Ⓓ They will initiate their project at the same time.

Let's **initiate** a parrot appreciation program!

4. In which sentence can *initial* fill in the blank?

Ⓕ My _____ are the same as yours.

Ⓖ The _____ season of the year is summer.

Ⓗ Saturday is the _____ last day of every week.

Ⓙ Breakfast is the _____ meal of the day for many people.

Writing Describe a *constructive* way to work out a problem between friends.
Use the word *constructive* in your writing.

_____

_____

_____

_____

absolute
absolutely
anticipate
anticipation
approximate
approximately
cohesive
compact
comparable
concise
condense
condensed
construct
constructive
debate
delete
deletion
discriminate
distinction
distinguish
expectation
foresee
formulate
initial
initiate
insert
insertion
issue
precede
preceding
prior
subsequent

Days 1–4

Each day's activity is a cloze paragraph that students complete with words or forms of words that they have learned in weeks 19–26. Before students begin, pronounce each word in the box on the student page, have students repeat each word, and then review each word's meaning(s). **Other ways to review the words:**

- Start a sentence containing one of the words and have students finish the sentence orally. For example:

  > *We can **anticipate** that today we will...*
  > *One example of **constructive** criticism is...*

- Provide students with a definition and ask them to supply the word that fits it.

- Ask questions that require students to know the meaning of each word. For example:

  > *How do you **discriminate** between answer choices on a test?*
  > *What are your **expectations** for next year?*

- Have students use each word in a sentence.

Day 5

Start by reviewing the words in the crossword puzzle activity for Day 5. Write the words on the board and have students repeat them after you. Provide a sentence for one of the words. Ask students to think of their own sentence and share it with a partner. Call on several students to share their sentences. Follow the same procedure for the remaining words. Then have students complete the crossword activity.

Extension Ideas

Use any of the following activities to help integrate the vocabulary words into other content areas:

- Have students examine a recent piece of writing. Ask them to look at each draft of their writing and identify **insertions** and **deletions** of information. Have students analyze their choices and decide on several generalizations of why they made those choices. Hold a **subsequent** group discussion to talk about those choices.

- Have students **formulate** an **initial** plan for a science fair project. They should make an **approximate** drawing of what they will **construct** and list their **expectations** of what they can learn from the project. Have students exchange plans and give **constructive** comments to a partner.

Name_____

| approximately | compact | concise | distinguish | initiated |
| cohesive | comparable | distinction | formulated | preceding |

Day 1

Fill in the blanks with words from the word box.

Papua New Guinea is a rugged and tropical country in Oceania. Not a

large country, it's _____ in size to the state of California.

_____ its independence in 1975, it was a colony of Australia.

A country known for its cultural diversity, a primary _____ is the

number of languages spoken there. There are _____

800 languages spoken in Papua New Guinea! It's amazing that there are so many

languages in such a small and _____ country!

Day 2

Fill in the blanks with words from the word box.

People _____ President Abraham Lincoln from other

historical figures not only because he ended slavery, but also because of his public

speaking skills. His "Gettysburg Address" is famous for its _____,

yet powerful, wording. This two-minute speech was _____ to

encourage the people of the United States to work together. At the time, the Civil

War was being fought and Americans were not a _____ people.

The speech _____ a new way of thinking about freedom and

similarities between all people, no matter what side of the war they were on.

Name _____

Daily
Academic
Vocabulary

| absolute | condense | debates | foresee | inserted | prior |
| anticipation | construct | delete | initial | issues | |

Day 3

Fill in the blanks with words from the word box.

For Earth Day this year, Ms. Jorgenson's class had a series of _____

on environmental subjects. _____ to the debates, teams were

assigned topics. One of the _____ was whether it was better to ask

for paper or plastic bags at the grocery store. Teams had a week to do research and

_____ their arguments. Many teams argued that more resources

are used in making paper bags. However, paper is more recyclable than plastic, so there

is no _____ answer. One team ultimately argued that a reusable cloth

bag was the best choice.

Day 4

Fill in the blanks with words from the word box.

Warren could _____ that the Web site was going to be a huge

success. He and a couple of friends had volunteered to _____, or

shorten, all of the information about the ski club and post it on the Internet. So far the Web

site had been a lot of hard work. In the _____ design, they ran out of

space for graphics. They had to _____ some of the text. Now the

graphics were _____ and the Web site was finished. The rest of the

ski club had been waiting in _____. They gave the Web site

designers a big round of applause.

Name _____

Daily
Academic
Vocabulary

Crossword Challenge

For each clue, write one of the words from the word box to complete the puzzle.

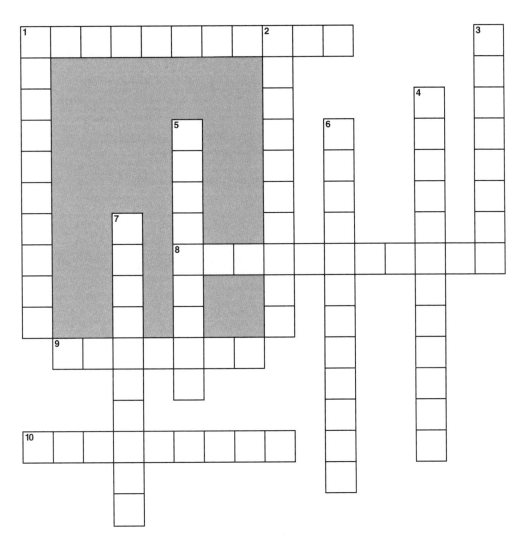

absolutely
anticipate
approximate
condensed
constructive
deletion
discriminate
expectation
insertion
precede
subsequent

Across

1. more or less correct or accurate
8. the belief that something will happen
9. to come before in time
10. an object or item that has been placed between two things

Down

1. to expect
2. completely
3. something that has been removed
4. to see a clear difference between things
5. shortened or made smaller
6. serving a useful purpose
7. coming next in time or order

integrate • integration
integral • inherent

Use the reproducible definitions on page 184 and the suggestions on page 6 to introduce the words for each day.

DAY 1

integrate
(verb) To combine things and make into a whole. *I will **integrate** many subplots into my story.*

Show students the comics page from your local paper. Ask: *What do comics **integrate**? What separate things are combined to form a comic?* (art and words) Then ask: *What separate things do we **integrate** to form a school day?* (e.g., different subjects; lunch) Encourage students to use the word **integrate** in their responses. Then have students complete the Day 1 activities on page 119. You may want to do the first one as a group.

DAY 2

integration
(noun) The act of combining all parts into a whole. *The **integration** of their group into ours will create one very strong team.*

Have students share their experiences with being part of the **integration** of smaller groups combined into a larger group, such as in group projects, schools, or teams. Ask: *What is involved in the process of **integration**?* (e.g., individuals or groups come together as equals) *Was **integration** helpful or harmful to the group?* Then have students complete the Day 2 activities on page 119. You may want to do the first one as a group.

DAY 3

integral
(adj.) Forming an essential part of something. *Teamwork is an **integral** part of any group project.*

Ask: *In what activities or situations is teamwork **integral**, or necessary, to success?* (e.g., sports; many jobs; families) *Why is it **integral**?* Then ask: *What are **integral** parts of family life?* (e.g., mealtimes; communicating) Have students use the word **integral** in their responses. Then have students complete the Day 3 activities on page 120. You may want to do the first one as a group.

DAY 4

inherent
(adj.) Being a core or inborn characteristic of something. *The student's **inherent** loyalty made him a good friend.*

Say: *If something is **inherent**, it is often an important or inborn quality of something.* Ask: *What other qualities are **inherent**, or essential, in a good friend?* (e.g., honesty; consideration) Then say: ***Inherent** also describes qualities that are inborn. For example, an **inherent** characteristic of cats is to hunt prey.* Then ask: *What are **inherent** characteristics of other animals?* (e.g., dogs barking; any predator or prey behavior) Encourage students to use the word **inherent** in their responses. Finally, have students complete the Day 4 activities on page 120. You may want to do the first one as a group.

DAY 5

Have students complete page 121. Call on students to read aloud their answers to the writing activity.

Daily Academic Vocabulary

Day 1 **integrate**

1. How would you complete this sentence? Say it aloud to a partner.

I would like to integrate _____ into my daily or weekly schedule.

2. The choir and band directors will *integrate* their ideas for the joint concert. What does that mean? Circle your answer.

a. The choir will have a concert instead of the band.
b. The band will have a concert instead of the choir.
c. The directors will combine their ideas into one concert.
d. The directors will compete to see who has the best ideas.

3. If a school decided to *integrate* the boys' and girls' soccer teams, which of these would be true? Circle your answer.

a. Some students would not be allowed to play.
b. There would not be enough coaches for everyone.
c. Both girls and boys would play separately.
d. Boys and girls would play on the same team.

4. How did your former teachers *integrate* learning with play?

_____

_____

Day 2 **integration**

1. How would you complete this sentence? Say it aloud to a partner.

The integration of various forms of technology into the classroom provides _____.

2. A newspaper reports on the successful *integration* of a small school into a larger school. What does that mean? Circle your answer.

a. A small school was opened.
b. A larger school got smaller.
c. A small school became part of a larger school.
d. Two schools were identified as the best for students.

3. Which word is an antonym for *integration*? Circle your answer.

a. connection   c. prediction
b. separation   d. rotation

Day 3 integral

1. How would you complete this sentence? Say it aloud to a partner.

_____ is an integral part of school for me because _____.

2. Which word would describe an *integral* subject in school? Circle your answer.

a. essential   c. unnecessary

b. optional   d. extra

3. In health class, you learn about habits that are *integral* to good health. What does that mean? Circle your answer.

a. You learn about habits that you need to break.

b. You learn not to worry about your health.

c. You learn about how to have a good health class.

d. You learn about critical habits to follow.

Day 4 inherent

1. How would you complete this sentence? Say it aloud to a partner.

I think that an inherent quality I have is _____.

2. If investigation is *inherent* in learning science, which of these is true? Circle your answer.

a. Science knowledge is not something you can learn.

b. Investigations are an essential part of learning science.

c. Scientists don't care about investigations.

d. Science learning requires facts but not investigations.

3. Which sentence does not use *inherent* correctly? Circle your answer.

a. Freedom is inherent in a democratic society.

b. Infants have the inherent ability to learn how to walk.

c. Physical risks are inherent in many sports.

d. Humor is inherent in all books.

4. What are *inherent* qualities of a good leader?

_____

_____

Name_____

Day 5 | integrate • integration • integral • inherent

Fill in the bubble next to the correct answer.

1. In which sentence could *integrate* fill in the blank?

Ⓐ We will _____ our activities into a family fitness plan.

Ⓑ Their family plans to _____ a vacation this summer.

Ⓒ One child will _____ swimming on the lake.

Ⓓ Another child wants to _____ how to water-ski.

2. In which sentence is *integration* used correctly?

Ⓕ The zoo animals are being fed with integration.

Ⓖ The zoo staff requires integration to be safe around the animals.

Ⓗ The integration of some animals means fewer separate cages.

Ⓙ The cages at the zoo were once a symbol of integration.

3. Which word is a synonym for *integral*?

Ⓐ persuasive

Ⓑ necessary

Ⓒ temporary

Ⓓ minor

4. In which sentence is *inherent* <u>not</u> used correctly?

Ⓕ She has an inherent friendliness.

Ⓖ Competition is an inherent part of sports activities.

Ⓗ Many of the band members have inherent talent in music.

Ⓙ There is an inherent that links good friends.

Good looks are **inherent** in parrots!

Writing   Describe an attitude or behavior that is *integral* to success in school. Be sure to use the word *integral* in your writing.

_____

_____

_____

_____

objective • subjective
bias • biased

Use the reproducible definitions on page 185 and the suggestions on page 6 to introduce the words for each day.

DAY 1

objective
(adj.) Based on fact, not feelings or opinions. *The judges were objective and chose the winner based on the quality of the entry.*

Say: *As a teacher, I need to be objective when grading your work. I do not base grades on feelings or opinions, but by how well you do on the task.* Ask: *Why is it important that I be objective? What other people need to be objective in their work?* (e.g., doctors; judges) *In what other situations do people need to be objective?* (e.g., giving awards; serving on a jury) Encourage students to use the word **objective** in their responses. Then have students complete the Day 1 activities on page 123. You may want to do the first one as a group.

DAY 2

subjective
(adj.) Based on feelings or opinions rather than on fact. *The judges were subjective and only looked at the entries they liked.*

Say: *Subjective is the opposite of "objective." If I was subjective when I graded your work, I would base your grades on my opinions of what I thought of you as a person.* Ask: *What are people often subjective about?* (e.g., friends; school; community) Students should use the word **subjective** in their answers. Then have students complete the Day 2 activities on page 123. You may want to do the first one as a group.

DAY 3

bias
(noun) A strong feeling for or against something that does not let someone be fair. *The contest shows a bias for students who have talent in music or art.*

Say: *When someone is subjective, they often have a bias for or against someone or something.* Ask: *How do people act when they show bias?* (e.g., kinder or meaner than normal; make judgments based on feeling) *In what situations do people often show bias?* (e.g., arguments; choosing teams; picking partners) Then have students complete the Day 3 activities on page 124. You may want to do the first one as a group.

DAY 4

biased
(adj.) Favoring or opposing one person, group, or point of view more than others. *The students were biased and believed their team was the best.*

Ask: *How would you behave if you were biased toward a specific team in a game?* (e.g., be more favorable to it; cheer for it) Discuss how people act if they are **biased** in their points of view. (e.g., don't listen to others) Then ask: *If someone was biased against you, what might they do or say?* Then have students complete the Day 4 activities on page 124. You may want to do the first one as a group.

DAY 5

Have students complete page 125. Call on students to read aloud their answers to the writing activity.

Name_____

Day 1 objective

1. **How would you complete this sentence? Say it aloud to a partner.**

   It is hard to be objective when _____.

2. **Which word would <u>not</u> describe an *objective* decision? Circle your answer.**

   a. fair   c. neutral

   b. angry   d. careful

3. **A newspaper reports on a problem in your community. What would be included in an *objective* article? Circle your answer.**

   a. a one-sided look at the problem

   b. an emotional description of the problem

   c. facts about the problem and different views of it

   d. how the newspaper can solve the problem

4. **In what situations do you find it hard to be *objective*? Why?**

   _____

   _____

Day 2 subjective

1. **How would you complete this sentence? Say it aloud to a partner.**

   I have a subjective opinion on _____.

2. **Which of these would be true of a *subjective* history of a country? Circle your answer.**

   a. It would be an accurate view of events.

   b. It would be a history told with just the facts.

   c. It would not contain anyone's opinion of events.

   d. It would be written from the author's point of view.

3. **Your teacher says that a report you wrote is too *subjective*. What does that mean? Circle your answer.**

   a. Your report is on a very interesting subject.

   b. Your penmanship looks like you were scribbling.

   c. You used too many facts and made your report dull.

   d. You expressed too many opinions and feelings in your report.

Day 3 bias

1. How would you complete this sentence? Say it aloud to a partner.

I have a bias for _____; I have a bias against _____.

2. Which of these would <u>not</u> be true of people who have a *bias* toward rock music? Circle your answer.

   a. They think rock music is about the same as other kinds.
   b. They like rock music more than other kinds.
   c. They pay attention to rock musicians more than other kinds.
   d. They go to more rock concerts than other kinds.

3. Your teacher asks you to look for *bias* in an article. What should you do? Circle your answer.

   a. Try to read faster.
   b. Check to see if the author is for or against someone or something.
   c. Check to see if the author of the article uses humor.
   d. Look for articles on the same subject to use for research.

Day 4 biased

1. How would you complete this sentence? Say it aloud to a partner.

I am biased against _____ because _____.

2. If a family is *biased* against beach vacations, which of these would be true? Circle your answer.

   a. The family has always had a great time on beach vacations.
   b. The family likes to go on vacations to the mountains.
   c. The family dislikes beach vacations for various reasons.
   d. The family does not like to go on any kind of vacation.

3. Which phrases would mean the opposite of *biased*? Circle your answers.

   a. open-minded   c. give and take
   b. come and go   d. middle of the road

4. Should newspapers be *biased*? Why or why not?

_____

_____

_____

Daily Academic Vocabulary

Day 5 **objective • subjective • bias • biased**

Fill in the bubble next to the correct answer.

1. In which sentence is *objective* used correctly?

Ⓐ They objective everything we suggest.

Ⓑ They are objective and look at both sides of the issue.

Ⓒ They are objective and spend more time with one friend than the other.

Ⓓ They are not objective and will always be late.

2. In which sentence could *subjective* fill in the blank?

Ⓕ I know I am _____, but I like our plan better.

Ⓖ We can be _____ that our plan was accepted.

Ⓗ You can organize a _____ day to discuss the plan.

Ⓙ They need a _____ way to be fair about the plan.

3. In which sentence is *bias* <u>not</u> used correctly?

Ⓐ Most people have a bias toward their own community.

Ⓑ Students may have a bias against other schools.

Ⓒ Teachers often have a bias toward their own subject.

Ⓓ Pets have a bias that allows them to like everyone.

*I have a **bias** toward birds!*

4. In which sentence could *biased* replace the underlined word or words?

Ⓕ The photo shows an <u>intricate</u> view of the planet Mars.

Ⓖ He prefers this song because he is <u>not equal</u> in his choices.

Ⓗ The CD includes <u>loud and strong</u> music that many people like.

Ⓙ We saw the play and were <u>not excited</u> by the lead actors.

Writing Describe a situation in which *bias* can be a good thing. Be sure to use the word *bias* in your writing.

_____

_____

_____

_____

speculate • speculation
hypothesize • hypothesis • theory

Use the reproducible definitions on page 186 and the suggestions on page 6 to introduce the words for each day.

DAY 1

speculate
(verb) To wonder or guess about something without knowing all the facts. *I can only speculate on my grade until I get my score.*

Say: *We speculate on many things throughout the day. I often speculate how many of you completed your homework.* Ask: *What things do you speculate about in school?* (e.g., how much homework you will get; what's for lunch) Then have students complete the Day 1 activities on page 127. You may want to do the first one as a group.

DAY 2

speculation
(noun) A conclusion that is reached by wondering and guessing without all the facts. *There is speculation about who will be chosen for the team.*

Say: *When you speculate, you make a speculation. For example, I speculate that it will rain today. Thinking that it will rain is my speculation.* Ask students to make their own speculations about what they will do next week. Have them begin with, "My speculation is ___." Then have students complete the Day 2 activities on page 127. You may want to do the first one as a group.

DAY 3

hypothesize
(verb) To make a guess based on some knowledge. *We can hypothesize that the rock will fall faster than the feather.*

hypothesis
(noun) A prediction or guess based on some knowledge. *Our hypothesis is that the rock will fall faster than the feather.*

Say: *When we hypothesize, we make an educated guess. That is, we make a guess based on some knowledge we have. When you hypothesize, you form a hypothesis.* Hold a pencil and a tissue. Ask: *If I drop these items at the same time, which do you hypothesize will hit the ground first?* Say: *Your hypothesis is that the ___ will hit the ground first when I drop them. I will test the hypothesis.* Then ask: *How do you hypothesize in science?* (guess based on what you know; when conducting experiments) *In reading?* (guess based on what you have already read) Then have students complete the Day 3 activities on page 128. You may want to do the first one as a group.

DAY 4

theory
(noun) A proposed explanation of something. *The global warming theory explains how the Earth's temperature is rising.*

Say: *"Hypothesis" and theory are synonyms. However, a theory is widely accepted by many people. It also has evidence to support it. Many studies and experiments must be done for a hypothesis to become a theory.* Give students ideas and ask if they could be scientific **theories**. Then ask why they could or could not be **theories**. Examples: *The moon is made of green cheese.* (no, has been proved false) *Greenhouse gases have caused a hole in the ozone layer.* (yes, can be proved) Then have students complete the Day 4 activities on page 128. You may want to do the first one as a group.

DAY 5

Have students complete page 129. Call on students to read aloud their answers to the writing activity.

Name_____

Day 1 speculate

1. **How would you complete this sentence? Say it aloud to a partner.**

   My friends and I often speculate about _____.

2. **Which word does not provide a clue to the meaning of speculate? Circle your answer.**

   a. question   c. assume

   b. guess   d. exclaim

3. **If you speculate about when the school picnic will be, which of these is true? Circle your answer.**

   a. You don't care about the picnic.

   b. You guess different days that the picnic will be held.

   c. You don't know if you want to go to the picnic.

   d. You know when the picnic will be, but you must keep it a secret.

4. **What do you speculate the next school year will be like?**

   _____

   _____

Day 2 speculation

1. **How would you complete this sentence? Say it aloud to a partner.**

   There is always speculation about _____ in our class.

2. **There is speculation that a movie will be filmed in your community. What does that mean? Circle your answer.**

   a. You should start looking for movie stars in your community.

   b. People in your community are not sure they like movies.

   c. Some people think that a movie will be filmed in your community.

   d. Everyone knows for sure that a movie will be filmed in your community.

3. **Which word is not a synonym for speculation? Circle your answer.**

   a. assumption   c. guess

   b. rumor   d. selection

Name_____

Day 3 | hypothesize • hypothesis

1. How would you complete these sentences? Say them aloud to a partner.

I hypothesize that my best friend will _____ as an adult.

To prove a hypothesis, I would need to _____.

2. Which sentence describes what you do when you *hypothesize?* Circle your answer.

    a. Make a careful prediction.   c. Look for a large size in something.

    b. Make a random guess.   d. Ask your teacher the answer.

3. Which statement does <u>not</u> describe a *hypothesis?* Circle your answer.

    a. It can be tested to determine if it is correct.

    b. It is known by everyone to be correct.

    c. It is a kind of prediction.

    d. It can proven true or false.

4. What do you *hypothesize* your future career will be? Why do you make that *hypothesis?*

_____

_____

_____

Day 4 | theory

1. How would you complete this sentence? Say it aloud to a partner.

I have heard of the scientific theory that explains _____.

2. What do scientists do to come up with *theories?* Circle your answer.

    a. propose to people   c. perform experiments

    b. guess reasons for things   d. explain why there are theories

3. What do you think the *theory* of flight does?

_____

_____

Name_____

Day 5 | speculate • speculation
hypothesize • hypothesis • theory

Fill in the bubble next to the correct answer.

1. In which sentence could *speculate* replace the underlined word?

Ⓐ We can <u>rotate</u> so that everyone gets to go first.

Ⓑ The doctor will <u>operate</u> the first thing in the morning.

Ⓒ The students all <u>wonder</u> about the first day of school.

Ⓓ They will <u>conduct</u> the first tours of the new museum.

2. In which sentence could *speculation* fill in the blank?

Ⓕ The _____ will take place in the morning.

Ⓖ The _____ is in charge of the new activities.

Ⓗ There will be _____ for all students who would like it.

Ⓙ There is _____ that a new coach will be introduced.

I **speculate** that you will answer these questions correctly.

3. In which sentence is *hypothesize* used correctly?

Ⓐ It is not likely that someone could hypothesize me.

Ⓑ The doctor can only hypothesize about the problem.

Ⓒ Their hypothesize does not sound accurate.

Ⓓ We will know better when the hypothesize is tested.

4. Which word gives a clue to the meaning of *theory*?

Ⓕ explanation

Ⓖ guess

Ⓗ clue

Ⓙ answer

Writing   Describe a *hypothesis* that you could make about homework for tonight.
Use at least one of this week's words in your writing.

_____

_____

_____

_____

WEEK
31

occasional • occasionally
intermittent • continuous • persistent

Use the reproducible definitions on page 187 and the suggestions on page 6 to introduce the words for each day.

DAY 1

occasional
(adj.) Happening from time to time. *We have an **occasional** assembly at school.*

occasionally
(adv.) From time to time. *We **occasionally** get to hear the chorus and band perform.*

Ask: *Who are some **occasional** visitors we have to our classroom?* (e.g., principal; visiting artists; parents) Say: *These are visitors that do not come every day, but from time to time. They visit our classroom **occasionally**.* Then ask: *What do we **occasionally** do in class?* (e.g., experiments; games) Encourage students to use the words **occasional** and **occasionally** in their responses. Have students complete the Day 1 activities on page 131. You may want to do the first one as a group.

DAY 2

intermittent
(adj.) Starting and stopping; not happening at regular times. *The school has visiting authors who work with students on an **intermittent** basis.*

Ask: *If rain is **intermittent**, what does it do?* (starts and stops) *If you make **intermittent** checks on a science experiment, when do you check it?* (at various times; not at regular times) Then have students complete the Day 2 activities on page 131. You may want to do the first one as a group.

DAY 3

continuous
(adj.) Going on without stopping. *Many people believe that learning should be **continuous** all through life.*

Say: *As a teacher, I have the **continuous** joy of watching students learn. This means that my enjoyment never stops.* Ask: *What things can be **continuous**?* (e.g., flow of water in streams; noise) Then have students name ways to make learning **continuous** through life. (e.g., take classes; read) Then have students complete the Day 3 activities on page 132. You may want to do the first one as a group.

DAY 4

persistent
(adj.) Lasting for a long time. *There is a **persistent** smell in the science lab that should be checked.*

(adj.) Refusing to give up or let go despite many challenges. *He is **persistent** and determined to succeed.*

Ask: *What things can be **persistent**, or last a long time?* Prompt students to think of weather and sounds if they have trouble with an answer. Be sure students understand that **persistent** implies that there is an end, though it may be long in coming, while "continuous" implies no end. Then ask: *What kinds of people are **persistent**?* (e.g., hard workers; salespeople; teachers) *When is it important to be **persistent**?* Then have students complete the Day 4 activities on page 132. You may want to do the first one as a group.

DAY 5

Have students complete page 133. Call on students to read aloud their answers to the writing activity.

Name_____

Daily Academic Vocabulary

1. How would you complete these sentences? Say them aloud to a partner.

_____ is an occasional activity that my family enjoys.

I see _____ occasionally but wish it were more often.

2. Which statement describes an *occasional* event? Circle your answer.

    a. It never happens.

    b. It has happened once in the past.

    c. It happens now and then.

    d. It happens every day.

3. Which phrase offers a clue to the meaning of *occasionally?* Circle your answer.

    a. once in a while   c. one to one

    b. once upon a time   d. once and for all

Day 2 intermittent

1. How would you complete this sentence? Say it aloud to a partner.

_____ is an intermittent activity for me because _____.

2. Which of these is true of an *intermittent* problem? Circle your answer.

    a. There is no pattern to when it occurs.

    b. It is impossible to solve.

    c. You get plenty of warning about the problem.

    d. It never comes back once you solve it.

3. If a cellphone provides *intermittent* service, which of these is true? Circle your answer.

    a. It works all the time.

    b. It works some times but not other times.

    c. It works every day for the same number of hours.

    d. It works whenever you make a call.

4. If someone has *intermittent* pain in his knees, when does it occur?

_____

_____

_____

**Daily
Academic
Vocabulary**

Day 3 continuous

1. How would you complete this sentence? Say it aloud to a partner.

I have a continuous desire to _____.

2. Which words are synonyms for *continuous*? Circle your answers.

a. nonstop   c. constant
b. onward   d. various

3. A teacher tells students to make a *continuous* effort to improve their writing skills. What does that mean? Circle your answer.

a. Students should do a few writing assignments during the year.
b. Students must write every second of the day.
c. Students should always be working to improve their skills.
d. Students should give up on trying to write anything.

Day 4 persistent

1. How would you complete these sentences? Say them aloud to a partner.

A persistent problem that some students have in school is _____.

I need to be persistent in order to _____.

2. If you have a *persistent* headache, which of these is true? Circle your answer.

a. It won't go away.   c. You hardly notice it.
b. It lasts for a very short time. d. It helps you think.

3. Your parent says that if you are *persistent,* you will find a way to go to college. What does that mean? Circle your answer.

a. Your parent has hidden money for you to find.
b. You should keep trying to find a way and not give up.
c. You should not bother trying to go to college.
d. You don't know where you want to go to college.

4. Describe a situation in which you were *persistent.*

_____

_____

Name_____

Daily Academic Vocabulary

Fill in the bubble next to the correct answer.

1. Which pair of words means the opposite of *occasional* and *occasionally*?

   Ⓐ seldom—never

   Ⓑ frequent—frequently

   Ⓒ rare—rarely

   Ⓓ ever—forever

2. In which sentence is *intermittent* used correctly?

   Ⓕ The lost boat sent an intermittent signal that would start and stop.

   Ⓖ The intermittent players were in every game.

   Ⓗ That song is intermittent on the radio and played all the time.

   Ⓙ The team has an intermittent schedule so they can plan ahead.

3. In which sentence could *continuous* fill in the blank?

   Ⓐ There are _____ people who can help.

   Ⓑ The children will volunteer for a _____ day.

   Ⓒ We will need a _____ bus to carry everyone.

   Ⓓ They have a _____ need for volunteers.

4. In which sentence could *persistent* replace the underlined words?

   Ⓕ We are <u>the best of</u> friends.

   Ⓖ The sound is <u>going on and on</u> and very loud.

   Ⓗ He is <u>full of fun</u> and makes us laugh.

   Ⓙ They saw a <u>long and boring</u> movie together.

*I show up **occasionally** in your lessons.*

Writing   When you have an obstacle to overcome, what helps you to be *persistent?* Be sure to use the word *persistent* in your writing.

_____

_____

_____

_____

WEEK 32

probable • plausible
feasible • potential

Use the reproducible definitions on page 188 and the suggestions on page 6 to introduce the words for each day.

DAY 1

probable
(adj.) Likely to happen or be true. *The **probable** outcome of the race will be a win for our team.*

Ask: *Why is **probable** different from the word "possible"?* Confirm that a possible event could happen but a **probable** event is likely to happen. Then ask: *What are the **probable** consequences of not brushing your teeth?* (e.g., cavities; plaque) *What is the **probable** cause of a sunburn?* (staying out in the sun too long) Say: *The opposite of **probable** is "improbable."* Ask: *What is an improbable cause of sunburn?* Then have students complete the Day 1 activities on page 135. You may want to do the first one as a group.

DAY 2

plausible
(adj.) Believable; likely, but not certain, to be true. *She gave a **plausible** excuse for not attending the ceremony.*

Ask: *Why is **plausible** different from "probable"?* (**plausible** is believable, but not certain; "probable" is likely to be true) Ask: *What are **plausible** reasons why students might not have their homework now and then?* (e.g., sickness; forgot it at home) Say: *The opposite of **plausible** is "implausible."* Ask: *What are implausible reasons why students might not have their homework?* Then have students complete the Day 2 activities on page 135. You may want to do the first one as a group.

DAY 3

feasible
(adj.) Capable of being done or brought about. *Finishing the project this week is a **feasible** objective.*

Say: *If something is **feasible**, it is able to be done.* Ask: *What are **feasible** goals for us to accomplish today?* (e.g., lunch; vocabulary lesson) Say: *Those are **feasible** goals because we can complete them today.* Ask: *What are <u>not</u> **feasible** goals for us to accomplish today?* (e.g., an entire unit; going to the moon) Then have students complete the Day 3 activities on page 136. You may want to do the first one as a group.

DAY 4

potential
(adj.) Able to come into being; possible. *The negotiators tried to avoid **potential** conflict between the two countries.*

Say: *If something is a **potential** problem, it could possibly become a problem.* Then ask: *If something is a **potential** solution, what does that mean?* (It could be a solution.) Ask: *What are **potential** school events that might occur this year?* (e.g., plays; field trips) Then have students complete the Day 4 activities on page 136. You may want to do the first one as a group.

DAY 5

Have students complete page 137. Call on students to read aloud their answers to the writing activity.

Name_____

Day 1 | probable

1. How would you complete this sentence? Say it aloud to a partner.

It is probable that my friends and I will _____ this week.

2. It is *probable* that a planned activity will be canceled because of bad weather. What does that mean? Circle your answer.

    a. There will be bad weather every day.

    b. There are too many activities planned and some should be canceled.

    c. An activity may happen that should be canceled.

    d. Most likely an activity will not happen because of weather.

3. If the *probable* cause of a fire was grease spilled on a stove, which of these is true? Circle your answer.

    a. Everyone agrees that spilled grease caused the fire for sure.

    b. The evidence points to a fire caused by spilled grease.

    c. No one has an idea about how the fire started.

    d. No one is sure if grease can catch on fire.

Day 2 | plausible

1. How would you complete this sentence? Say it aloud to a partner.

It is plausible that I can accomplish _____ by the end of this year.

2. Scientists disagree about whether a particular theory is *plausible*. What are they disagreeing about? Circle your answer.

    a. if the theory exists

    b. if the theory could be true

    c. if anyone knows about the theory

    d. if anyone cares about the theory

3. Which statement is true of a *plausible* explanation? Circle your answer.

    a. It cannot be understood or believed.

    b. No one agrees with it.

    c. It is full of errors.

    d. It is reasonable and can be believed.

It's completely **plausible** that I am the smartest parrot I know.

Daily Academic Vocabulary

Day 3 feasible

1. How would you complete this sentence? Say it aloud to a partner.

A feasible project to complete in a weekend is _____.

2. Which of these is a *feasible* job for a person your age? Circle your answer.

   a. caring for a pet
   b. performing surgery
   c. teaching high school
   d. running a company

3. In which sentence is *feasible* not used correctly? Circle your answer.

   a. A feasible field trip is to visit the art museum two blocks away.
   b. A feasible homework assignment is to write a book by tomorrow.
   c. A feasible expectation of students is for them to try their very best.
   d. A feasible way to get exercise is to join a sports team.

4. Describe a *feasible* goal you can accomplish this summer.

_____

_____

Day 4 potential

1. How would you complete this sentence? Say it aloud to a partner.

A potential goal I can accomplish this year is _____.

2. Which statements are not true of a *potential* activity? Circle your answers.

   a. It cannot happen.
   b. It could happen.
   c. It might happen.
   d. It will definitely happen.

3. In which sentence is *potential* used correctly? Circle your answer.

   a. The potential event will definitely occur.
   b. A potential result of the experiment is that the magnet will attract the nail.
   c. The student has a potential that she will add to the discussion.
   d. Some potentials will affect the outcome of the election.

Name_____

Day 5 probable • plausible • feasible • potential

Fill in the bubble next to the correct answer.

1. In which sentence is _probable_ used correctly?

Ⓐ My probable summer vacation is over.

Ⓑ A probable meeting took place yesterday.

Ⓒ Our probable favorite activity is soccer.

Ⓓ A probable reason for the delay is the rain.

2. Which phrase is a clue to the meaning of _plausible_?

Ⓕ won't happen

Ⓖ not likely to happen

Ⓗ can imagine it happening

Ⓙ it will happen

It is **plausible** that you will earn a perfect score today!

3. In which sentence is _feasible_ used correctly?

Ⓐ He was feasible that he could do it.

Ⓑ It's not feasible to build the model in two days.

Ⓒ No one knows what will happen in the feasible.

Ⓓ Humor is a feasible of this author's writing.

4. In which sentence could _potential_ fill in the blank?

Ⓕ We know the _____ party will take place.

Ⓖ The _____ thunderstorm caused flooding.

Ⓗ The bad weather may be a _____ problem.

Ⓙ It is _____ and unusual to see them here.

Writing   Explain the difference between a _probable_ cause and a _plausible_ cause
of an accident. Be sure to use the words _probable_ and _plausible_ in your writing.

_____

_____

_____

_____

cite • citation
assert • validate

Use the reproducible definitions on page 189 and the suggestions on page 6 to introduce the words for each day.

DAY 1

cite
(verb) To refer to for explanation or proof. *I always **cite** the sources that I use in my reports.*

Say: *When you give credit to a source of information you use in a report or essay, you **cite** that source by saying who originally wrote that information. Why do you think you should **cite** someone else's work if you use it in your own?* (e.g., so people don't think those are your own ideas) Then have students complete the Day 1 activities on page 139. You may want to do the first one as a group.

DAY 2

citation
(noun) A short note recognizing a source of information or of a quoted passage. *The **citation** of the history book informed the reader where the writer found her information.*

Say: *A **citation** is what you make when you cite a source of information. There are many forms of **citations**. You can say within your writing who wrote the information. You can also create a separate page listing your information sources.* Then say: *A **citation** helps the reader of an essay to know where you found your information. It also gives credit to the original author.* Ask: *Have you ever seen a **citation**? Where?* (e.g., literature and history textbooks) Show forms of **citations** if available. Then have students complete the Day 2 activities on page 139. You may want to do the first one as a group.

DAY 3

assert
(verb) To state or declare strongly. *We need to **assert** our support of our friend.*

Point out that **assert** implies having strong feelings or doing something boldly and confidently. Ask: *How can you **assert** support for a friend? How can you **assert** your opinion? Have you ever **asserted** something? What was it?* Be sure students use the word **assert** when they respond. Then have students complete the Day 3 activities on page 140. You may want to do the first one as a group.

DAY 4

validate
(verb) To prove true or factual; to confirm by giving evidence or support. *The research I found **validates** my idea.*

Say: *When something can prove your idea to be true, it **validates** your idea. When writing an essay or report, you often want to cite sources that **validate** your views. Why do you think this would help support your views? What kinds of sources would **validate** your ideas?* Encourage students to use the word **validate** in their responses. Then have students complete the Day 4 activities on page 140. You may want to do the first one as a group.

DAY 5

Have students complete page 141. Call on students to read aloud their answers to the writing activity.

**Daily
Academic
Vocabulary**

Day 1 cite

1. How would you complete this sentence? Say it aloud to a partner.

Some references that I might cite for a report are _____.

2. Which statement is true when you *cite* a source? Circle your answer.

   a. You give credit to someone else's ideas.
   b. You are repeating a rumor.
   c. You don't believe the information is worth repeating.
   d. You can't see the source's point of view.

3. Which sentence describes someone *citing* a source? Circle your answer.

   a. Renita asked her teacher to repeat the directions.
   b. Chloe did not write down the author and title of the article in which she found the data.
   c. Gavin told his audience who said the quotation he repeated.
   d. Tayshaun read an article from the encyclopedia.

Day 2 citation

1. How would you complete this sentence? Say it aloud to a partner.

A citation of a newspaper article would probably include _____.

2. Which sentence uses *citation* correctly? Circle your answer.

   a. William always citations his sources.
   b. Scott's citation told us where to meet him for the study group.
   c. My citation is that you should always give credit to other authors.
   d. Emily's essay failed to list several important citations.

3. Why do you think there is so much emphasis on including *citations* in your writing?

_____

_____

_____

_____

Day 3 assert

1. How would you complete this sentence? Say it aloud to a partner.

I assert my opinion when _____.

2. In history, you read about a colony trying to *assert* its independence. What does that mean? Circle your answer.

    a. The colony is trying to avoid becoming independent.

    b. The colony is losing a war for independence.

    c. The colony is declaring its right to be independent.

    d. The colony is a place where people can be free.

3. If you *assert* your point of view on a topic, which of these is true? Circle your answer.

    a. No one knows what you think about the topic.

    b. You are not interested in the topic.

    c. You don't really have a point of view.

    d. Others know exactly what you think about the topic.

4. Why is it important to *assert* your opinions?

_____

_____

Day 4 validate

1. How would you complete this sentence? Say it aloud to a partner.

I could validate my view on an issue by _____.

2. Which of these things would *validate* global warming? Circle your answer.

    a. Statistics and evidence that show an increase in the temperature of the Earth.

    b. Statistics and evidence that show a decrease in the temperature of the Earth.

    c. A famous person saying he or she believes in global warming.

    d. People talking about how it feels warmer this year than last year.

3. Which sentence correctly uses *validate*? Circle your answer.

    a. You should validate your thoughts with mine.

    b. In order to validate my theory, I disproved it.

    c. The experiment should validate the idea that exercise lowers blood pressure.

    d. What kind of validate do I need to support my views?

Name_____

Day 5 cite • citation • assert • validate

Fill in the bubble next to the correct answer.

1. In which sentence is _cite_ used correctly?

Ⓐ Find the cite of the restaurant on the map.

Ⓑ We have no way to cite which is the best restaurant to try.

Ⓒ We can call this restaurant to cite what kind of food they serve.

Ⓓ We can cite this restaurant as an example of a good place to eat.

2. In which sentence is _citation_ used correctly?

Ⓕ I can citation several reviews that say the movie is awful.

Ⓖ Please include a citation to support your argument.

Ⓗ There is no way to citation how this book will end.

Ⓙ We can citation a famous quote to introduce our presentation.

3. In which sentence could _assert_ fill in the blank?

Ⓐ We _____ that we need more time to complete the project.

Ⓑ The _____ of his painting was excellent.

Ⓒ They need an _____ to prove their experiment can work.

Ⓓ We shyly _____ our question to the teacher.

4. Which word is a clue to the meaning of _validate_?

Ⓕ give

Ⓖ support

Ⓗ write

Ⓙ find

I **assert** that parrots are the best birds of all!

Writing What could you use to _validate_ your opinion on the necessity of doing well in school? Use at least one of this week's words in your writing.

_____

_____

_____

_____

explicit • implicit
denotation • connotation

Use the reproducible definitions on page 190 and the suggestions on page 6 to introduce the words for each day.

DAY 1

explicit
(adj.) Very clearly stated; precise. *We received* **explicit** *instructions for the assignment.*

Ask: *What would* **explicit** *instructions be like?* (e.g., very detailed; explaining exactly what to do) *What would an* **explicit** *warning be like?* (e.g., very clear warning) *Can you give me some examples of* **explicit** *warnings?* Then have students complete the Day 1 activities on page 143. You may want to do the first one as a group.

DAY 2

implicit
(adj.) Not stated but understood in what is said; implied. *It was* **implicit** *from the instructions that the assignment was important and should be done carefully.*

Ask: *What does "explicit" mean?* Then introduce **implicit** as its opposite. Refer to the sample sentence. Ask: *What is* **implicit** *from the instructions?* (e.g., the assignment is important and to be done carefully) Discuss clues that communicate **implicit** messages. (e.g., tone of voice or writing; choice of words) Then have students complete the Day 2 activities on page 143. You may want to do the first one as a group.

DAY 3

denotation
(noun) The most specific, exact meaning of a word or expression. *The* **denotation** *of the word "school" is a place where students are taught.*

Point out that the **denotation** of a word is the dictionary definition. Give an example of a common expression, such as "awesome." Have a student look up the definition in a dictionary and read it aloud. (e.g., "inspiring awe") Say: *That is the* **denotation** *of the word "awesome." That is exactly what it means.* Point out that many words carry another meaning, which they will learn about on Day 4. Then have students complete the Day 3 activities on page 144. You may want to do the first one as a group.

DAY 4

connotation
(noun) An additional meaning associated with or suggested by a word besides the exact meaning. *For many students, the* **connotation** *of "school" is the place where they see their friends.*

Introduce **connotation** as the "additional meaning" referred to on Day 3. Point out that the **connotation** is what the word brings to mind based on personal associations or by common usage. Give the example of "awesome." Have students state their **connotation** of "awesome." (e.g., something amazing; "really cool") Then have one student recall from Day 3 or look in the dictionary for the definition of "awesome." Discuss how the denotation and **connotation** of words differ. Ask: *Can you think of any words that have different denotations and* **connotations**? (e.g., "cool"; "neat"; "hot") Then have students complete the Day 4 activities on page 144. You may want to do the first one as a group.

DAY 5

Have students complete page 145. Call on students to read aloud their answers to the writing activity.

Daily Academic Vocabulary • EMC 2762 • © Evan-Moor Corp.

Name_____

Day 1 explicit

1. **How would you complete this sentence? Say it aloud to a partner.**

   An explicit request that I might hear from a teacher is _____.

2. **If your parent asks you to be more *explicit* about your plans with friends, what do you need to do? Circle your answer.**

   a. Don't go into so much detail.
   b. State more clearly what you plan to do.
   c. Give a reason why you have plans.
   d. Explain why you like to be with friends.

3. **Which word is <u>not</u> a clue to the meaning of *explicit*? Circle your answer.**

   a. detailed   c. precise
   b. specific   d. unclear

4. **Give *explicit* directions from the classroom door to your desk.**

   _____

   _____

Day 2 implicit

1. **How would you complete this sentence? Say it aloud to a partner.**

   An implicit message that kids can get from adults is _____.

2. **Your history teacher asks what is *implicit* when taking a test. How could you respond? Circle your answers.**

   a. You are to copy the answers from another student.
   b. You are to talk during the test.
   c. You are to write legibly.
   d. You are to do your own work.

3. **Which word is a clue to the meaning of *implicit*? Circle your answer.**

   a. imitated   c. important
   b. implied   d. intended

It's **implicit** from my scholarly words that I'm a very intelligent bird.

**Daily
Academic
Vocabulary**

Day 3 denotation

1. How would you complete this sentence? Say it aloud to a partner.

The denotation of the saying "Don't judge a book by its cover" is _____.

**2. A test question gives a word and asks you to choose the *denotation.*
What do you need to do? Circle your answer.**

   a. Choose a picture of the word.
   b. Choose a sentence using the word.
   c. Choose the exact definition of the word.
   d. Choose what the word reminds you of.

3. Which statement would be true of the *denotation* of an expression? Circle your answer.

   a. It is the precise meaning of the expression.
   b. It is the common way some people use the expression.
   c. It is finding a new way to use the expression.
   d. It is describing the experience of using the expression.

4. Why should you learn the *denotation* of words?

_____

_____

Day 4 connotation

1. How would you complete this sentence? Say it aloud to a partner.

The connotation of the saying "Don't judge a book by its cover" is _____.

**2. If a science teacher asks students to explain their *connotation* of the word "science,"
which of these is <u>not</u> true? Circle your answer.**

   a. The teacher wants to find out if students can define "science."
   b. The teacher wants to find out how students feel about science.
   c. The teacher is checking for activities students connect with science.
   d. The teacher is checking for ideas students associate with science.

3. Which of these do you get from the *connotation* of a word? Circle your answer.

   a. the exact meaning   c. what the word suggests
   b. the proper use of the word   d. how the word is pronounced

Name_____

Daily Academic Vocabulary

Day 5 explicit • implicit • denotation • connotation

Fill in the bubble next to the correct answer.

1. Which word is a synonym for *explicit*?

Ⓐ exciting

Ⓑ sharp

Ⓒ precise

Ⓓ successful

2. In which sentence is *implicit* used correctly?

Ⓕ The implicit message was stated very clearly.

Ⓖ It was implicit by her tone of voice that she was pleased.

Ⓗ If you implicit your feelings, I will understand them better.

Ⓙ No one understands their implicit vocabulary.

3. In which sentence could *denotation* fill in the blank?

Ⓐ The _____ of the word is easy to find with the right resource.

Ⓑ We will need music to _____ the meaning of this word.

Ⓒ There is a _____ of several words to consider when you edit.

Ⓓ There is no need to _____ that word for this assignment.

4. In which sentence is *connotation* <u>not</u> used correctly?

Ⓕ His connotation of "friend" is different from mine.

Ⓖ My connotation of "fun" is not this kind of activity.

Ⓗ Let's check the dictionary for the connotation of "freedom."

Ⓙ Our connotation of a word is influenced by personal experiences.

Writing Explain your *connotation* of the expression "way to go." How is that different from its *denotation?* Be sure to use at least one of this week's words in your writing.

_____

_____

_____

relevant • irrelevant • appropriate
pertain • pertinent

Use the reproducible definitions on page 191 and the suggestions on page 6 to introduce the words for each day.

DAY 1

relevant
(adj.) Having to do with what is currently being discussed or is important. *Knowing the last day of school is relevant to making our summer vacation plans.*

irrelevant
(adj.) Not having to do with what is being considered or discussed. *The date of winter break is irrelevant to making our summer plans.*

Ask: *What other information is relevant to making vacation plans?* (e.g., knowing where you want to go) *What information would be relevant to taking a test?* (e.g., knowing what the test covers) Then show students how adding the prefix "ir-" creates the opposite, **irrelevant**. Ask: *What information is irrelevant to making summer vacation plans?* (e.g., when Thanksgiving is) *What information is irrelevant to taking a test?* (e.g., the color of the paper) Discuss other things that are **relevant** and **irrelevant** to school. Then have students complete the Day 1 activities on page 147. You may want to do the first one as a group.

DAY 2

appropriate
(adj.) Suitable, or right for the purpose. *It is appropriate that all students who made an extra effort should receive an award.*

Have students identify **appropriate** school behavior. Then ask: *Why it is appropriate to be honored for extra effort?* (e.g., because students have worked hard) Discuss other things that are **appropriate**. (e.g., level of noise in a library) Then say: *The opposite of appropriate is "inappropriate." What are inappropriate behaviors at the dinner table?* Have students complete the Day 2 activities on page 147. You may want to do the first one as a group.

DAY 3

pertain
(verb) To relate to or have to do with something. *Those materials all pertain to geometry.*

Gather books, paper, pencils, and pens. Show students the objects and ask how they are alike. Say: *All of these pertain, or relate to, reading and writing.* Discuss how the academic vocabulary lessons **pertain** to school and beyond. Have students complete the Day 3 activities on page 148. You may want to do the first one as a group.

DAY 4

pertinent
(adj.) Having to do with or connected to a subject. *That book is pertinent to our discussion of books to read this summer.*

Help students connect **pertinent** with "pertain" from Day 3. Then ask: *What topics are pertinent to school discussions?* (e.g., current events; scientific discoveries) *What are examples of questions or topics that could be pertinent to academic vocabulary?* Then have students complete the Day 4 activities on page 148. You may want to do the first one as a group.

DAY 5

Have students complete page 149. Call on students to read aloud their answers to the writing activity.

Daily Academic Vocabulary • EMC 2762 • © Evan-Moor Corp.

Daily Academic Vocabulary

Day 1 relevant • irrelevant

1. How would you complete these sentences? Say them aloud to a partner.

Something that is relevant to doing well in school is _____.

Something that is irrelevant to doing well in school is _____.

2. A teacher asks you to choose a *relevant* topic for a report. What does that mean? Circle your answer.

   a. You can choose any topic you like.
   b. The topic needs to relate to what you are studying.
   c. The topic needs to require a lot of research.
   d. Everyone is supposed to choose the same topic.

3. A teacher says that your report has *irrelevant* information. What does that mean? Circle your answer.

   a. Everything you included in your report is important.
   b. You included interesting information in your report.
   c. You didn't do as much research as your teacher requested.
   d. You included information that is not connected to your topic.

Day 2 appropriate

1. How would you complete this sentence? Say it aloud to a partner.

An appropriate way to treat a new student in school is to _____.

2. If a movie is *appropriate* for all ages, which of these is true? Circle your answer.

   a. Only children can see it.
   b. Only adults can see it.
   c. The movie is suitable for anyone to see.
   d. The movie is about people of all ages.

3. Your teacher praises the class because everyone has the *appropriate* materials for an activity. What does that mean? Circle your answer.

   a. Everyone has the right materials for the activity.
   b. Everyone has done a great job on the activity.
   c. Everyone has the oldest materials they could find.
   d. Everyone has exciting materials to share.

I always know the **appropriate** thing to say.

**Daily
Academic
Vocabulary**

Day 3 pertain

1. How would you complete this sentence? Say it aloud to a partner.

My favorite kinds of books pertain to _____.

2. Your teacher says that test questions will *pertain* to stories you have read this year. What does that mean? Circle your answer.

    a. The test questions will cover many subjects.

    b. The test questions will be about stories you have read.

    c. The test will have stories to read and questions to answer.

    d. You cannot study for the test.

3. If most of your summer activities *pertain* to being outdoors, which of these is true? Circle your answer.

    a. You don't care where you are in the summer.

    b. You spend a lot of time indoors in the summer.

    c. You like to read about and watch different summer activities.

    d. Your summer activities primarily take place outside.

Day 4 pertinent

1. How would you complete this sentence? Say it aloud to a partner.

Something that is pertinent to preparing for my future education is _____.

2. Which word is a clue to the meaning of *pertinent?* Circle your answer.

    a. related   c. indifferent

    b. determined   d. separate

3. Which statement is true of a *pertinent* question? Circle your answer.

    a. It is a trick question and has no answer.

    b. It is a rude question.

    c. It has to do with what is being studied or discussed.

    d. It has to do with a topic that should not be discussed.

4. Why would it be important to have *pertinent* resources when you are writing a report?

_____

_____

Name_____

Fill in the bubble next to the correct answer.

1. Which phrase is a clue to the meaning of *irrelevant*?

Ⓐ point of view

Ⓑ not to the point

Ⓒ to the point

Ⓓ point out

2. Which phrase means the opposite of *appropriate*?

Ⓕ out of place

Ⓖ out loud

Ⓗ up and down

Ⓙ suitable to

3. In which sentence could *pertain* fill in the blank?

Ⓐ The letters do not _____ a large folder to hold them.

Ⓑ The letters _____ many adventures.

Ⓒ The letters _____ ideas that we can discuss.

Ⓓ The letters _____ to our report on famous diarists.

4. Which sentence uses *pertinent* correctly?

Ⓕ A pertinent problem is connected to a situation and needs to be solved.

Ⓖ A pertinent answer has nothing to do with the question that was asked.

Ⓗ A pertinent discussion is not connected to any subject.

Ⓙ A pertinent activity is just for fun and can be done anytime.

Writing   Think of a question you have that is *relevant* to what you are studying
in school. Where can you find answers that *pertain* to your question?
Be sure to use at least one of this week's words in your response.

_____

_____

_____

_____

CUMULATIVE REVIEW
WORDS FROM WEEKS 28–35

appropriate
assert
bias
biased
citation
cite
connotation
continuous
denotation
explicit
feasible
hypothesis
hypothesize
implicit
inherent
integral
integrate
integration
intermittent
irrelevant
objective
occasional
occasionally
persistent
pertain
pertinent
plausible
potential
probable
relevant
speculate
speculation
subjective
theory
validate

Days 1–4

Each day's activity is a cloze paragraph that students complete with words or forms of words that they have learned in weeks 28–35. Before students begin, pronounce each word in the box on the student page, have students repeat each word, and then review each word's meaning(s). **Other ways to review the words:**

- Start a sentence containing one of the words and have students finish the sentence orally. For example:

  *A **feasible** expectation of all students is…*
  *In school, we **occasionally**…*

- Provide students with a definition and ask them to supply the word that fits it.

- Ask questions that require students to know the meaning of each word. For example:

  *Would an **irrelevant** problem be important to solve? Why or why not?*
  *What are ways that teachers sometimes **integrate** subjects?*

- Have students use each word in a sentence.

Day 5

Start by reviewing the fourteen words not practiced on Days 1–4: **bias**, **biased**, **citation**, **cite**, **denotation**, **hypothesize**, **integration**, **intermittent**, **irrelevant**, **occasional**, **pertain**, **plausible**, **theory**, and **validate**. Write the words on the board and have students repeat them after you. Provide a sentence for one of the words. Ask students to think of their own sentence and share it with a partner. Call on several students to share their sentences. Follow the same procedure for the remaining words. Then have students complete the code-breaker activity.

Extension Ideas

Use any of the following activities to help integrate the vocabulary words into other content areas:

- Have students create their own cloze paragraphs using the words not practiced on Days 1–4 of this week. Have them trade paragraphs and try to complete each other's paragraphs.

- Have students create personal word lists that identify both the **denotation** and **connotation** of words from different subject areas and everyday speech.

- Start a "quotation of the day" and have students take turns **citing** quotations that are **relevant** to different subject areas. Encourage them to **assert** why that quotation is **relevant**.

Daily Academic Vocabulary • EMC 2762 • © Evan-Moor Corp.

Name _____

asserted	connotation	feasible	inherent	occasionally	relevant
continuous	hypothesis	integrated	persistent	speculate	

Day 1

Fill in the blanks with words from the word box.

Tenzing Norgay was certain of one thing while he was growing up. Someday,

the sherpa would stand on the top of Mt. Everest! Most people didn't believe

it _____ to climb to 29,028 feet above sea level. But besides

being born with _____ courage and determination, Tenzing was

_____. It wasn't until his seventh try that he succeeded in climbing

Mt. Everest! On May 29, 1953, he and Edmund Hillary were the first people to stand

at the top of the tallest mountain in the world. Although a "sherpa" is still known as

a cultural group in Nepal, the word has another _____ today—

a mountain climber!

Day 2

Fill in the blanks with words from the word box.

Mr. Johnson asked us for questions _____ to science. After

Lupe asked why the sky looks blue, Mr. Johnson asked us to _____

on her question. I guessed that it had to do with light moving through air. Joe had a

_____ that was more specific. He _____ that light

appears white but is really several _____ colors. It usually moves in

a straight and _____ line. But _____ it bumps into

a bit of dust or gas. Then the light bounces off and breaks into individual colors. Blue

is simply the color we see most.

Daily Academic Vocabulary

appropriate	implicit	objective	potential	speculation
explicit	integral	pertinent	probable	subjective

Day 3

Fill in the blanks with words from the word box.

If you see paper dragons and red decorations in late January or early February,

it is _____ that they are for Chinese New Year. This holiday is an

_____ part of Chinese culture. It is an _____

time to shoot off fireworks and eat special foods. Some think the holiday began to

celebrate the start of spring. Another _____ of folklore is that

an aggressive beast chased people every new year. People used the color red and

fireworks to scare it away. Of course, that explanation is _____,

as opposed to factual. No matter the reason, though, it's an exciting time of the year!

Day 4

Fill in the blanks with words from the word box.

Before Ms. Diaz left, she gave clear and _____ directions

to write a paragraph for each question on the board. Those directions eliminated

_____ questions. She didn't have to remind the students to do their

best, either. It was _____ every time she assigned a task. When

the students came to the final question, they were surprised because it wasn't very

factual or _____. It was, "What is the most beautiful dessert?"

Usually the questions were _____ to geography. When Ms. Diaz

returned, she looked at the board, started laughing, and exclaimed, "I guess even

teachers make mistakes!" She meant to write "desert," not "dessert"!

Name_____

Crack the Code!

Write one of the words from the word box on the lines next to each clue.

appropriate	continuous	integral	occasionally	relevant
assert	denotation	integrate	persistent	speculate
assertion	explicit	integration	pertain	speculation
bias	hypothesis	intermittent	pertinent	subjective
biased	hypothesize	irrelevant	plausible	theory
cite	implicit	objective	possible	validate
connotation	inherent	occasional	probable	

1. stopping and starting   __ __ __ __ __ __ __ __ __ __ __ __
                                              1

2. happening from time to time   __ __ __ __ __ __ __ __ __ __
                                                   2

3. believable   __ __ __ __ __ __ __ __ __
                        3   4

4. to refer to for explanation or proof   __ __ __ __
                                                        5

5. to have to do with   __ __ __ __ __ __ __
                                  6

6. the exact meaning of a word or an expression   __ __ __ __ __ __ __ __ __ __
                                                                        7

7. to prove true or factual   __ __ __ __ __ __ __ __
                                        8

8. a strong feeling that does not let someone be fair   __ __ __ __
                                                                        9

Now use the numbers under the letters to crack the code. Write the letters on the lines below.
The words will answer this question:

Why did George Mallory say he wanted to climb Mt. Everest in 1924?

" __ __ __ __ __ __ __   __ __   __ __   __ h __ __ __ ."
    4 7 2 8 3 9 7   1 5   1 9   5   7 6 7

Answer Key

Week 1

Day 1
2. c
3. a

Day 2
2. b
3. Answers will vary.

Day 3
2. d
3. d

Day 4
2. c
3. a

Day 5
1. D   2. F   3. B   4. H

Week 2

Day 1
2. d
3. b

Day 2
2. c
3. a, b

Day 3
2. c, d, b, a
3. Answers will vary.

Day 4
2. a
3. b

Day 5
1. D   2. G   3. A   4. H

Week 3

Day 1
2. b
3. a
4. Answers will vary.

Day 2
2. c
3. d

Day 3
2. b
3. c

Day 4
2. d
3. a

Day 5
1. D   2. F   3. C   4. G

Week 4

Day 1
2. b
3. d

Day 2
2. c
3. a

Day 3
2. c
3. a

Day 4
2. d
3. b

Day 5
1. A   2. H   3. D   4. G

Week 5

Day 1
2. a
3. b
4. Answers will vary.

Day 2
2. d
3. b

Day 3
2. d
3. c

Day 4
2. a
3. d
4. Answers will vary.

Day 5
1. D   2. G   3. C   4. F

Week 6

Day 1
2. d
3. c
4. Answers will vary.

Day 2
2. b
3. a

Day 3
2. d
3. a

Day 4
2. a
3. b
4. Answers will vary.

Day 5
1. B   2. J   3. C   4. F

Week 7

Day 1
2. Answers will vary.
3. c

Day 2
2. d
3. Answers will vary.

Day 3
2. b, c
3. Answers will vary.
4. Answers will vary.

Day 4
2. a, b
3. a

Day 5
1. A   2. H   3. B   4. H

Week 8

Day 1
2. b
3. Answers will vary.

Day 2
2. d
3. a
4. Answers will vary.

Day 3
2. b
3. c
4. Answers will vary.

Day 4
2. b
3. c
4. light, water, food

Daily Academic Vocabulary • EMC 2762 • © Evan-Moor Corp.

Day 5

1. C 2. J 3. A 4. H

Week 9 Review

Day 1

inconceivable, vital, characteristic, minimal, establish

Day 2

narrative, dissimilar, characterized, essentials, intended

Day 3

proposition, options, minimum, intention, equivalent

Day 4

proposed, property, identical, unique, concept, demonstration

Day 5

Across

1. exaggerate
4. proposal
9. narration
11. trait
12. minimize

Down

1. exaggeration
2. optional
3. conceptualize
5. demonstrate
6. character
7. conceive
8. narrate
10. narrator

Week 10

Day 1

2. c
3. a
4. Answers will vary.

Day 2

2. b
3. c, d
4. Answers will vary.

Day 3

2. c
3. d

Day 4

2. a
3. b
4. Answers will vary.

Day 5

1. C 2. G 3. D 4. F

Week 11

Day 1

2. d
3. b

Day 2

2. a
3. b
4. Answers will vary.

Day 3

2. c
3. d

Day 4

2. a
3. c

Day 5

1. D 2. H 3. A 4. G

Week 12

Day 1

2. b
3. d

Day 2

2. c
3. a

Day 3

2. c
3. b

Day 4

2. d
3. c
4. Answers will vary.

Day 5

1. C 2. G 3. B 4. F

Week 13

Day 1

2. c
3. b

Day 2

2. a
3. d
4. Answers will vary.

Day 3

2. c
3. a

Day 4

2. c
3. b
4. Answers will vary.

Day 5

1. C 2. F 3. D 4. G

Week 14

Day 1

2. c
3. d
4. Answers will vary.

Day 2

2. b
3. c

Day 3

2. b
3. b

Day 4

2. c
3. d

Day 5

1. B 2. J 3. C 4. F

Week 15

Day 1

2. c
3. b

Day 2

2. d
3. a
4. Answers will vary.

Day 3

2. a
3. c

Day 4

2. d
3. b
4. Answers will vary.

Day 5

1. A 2. H 3. D 4. G

Week 16

Day 1
2. c
3. a
4. Answers will vary.

Day 2
2. b
3. d

Day 3
2. Answers will vary.
3. d

Day 4
2. a
3. c

Day 5
1. B   2. J   3. C   4. J

Week 17

Day 1
2. c
3. b
4. Answers will vary.

Day 2
2. d
3. a

Day 3
2. d
3. b

Day 4
2. c
3. b
4. Answers will vary.

Day 5
1. B   2. H   3. A   4. H

Week 18 Review

Day 1
former, latter, classified, accumulates

Day 2
classifications, strategy, acquiring, manner, omission, excludes

Day 3
infer, analyzed, systematic, compiled, account for

Day 4
account, system, involved, version, omitted

Day 5
1. accumulation
2. analysis
3. contemplate
4. surmise
5. inference
6. procedure
7. strategic
8. strategize
code: cut hard metals

Week 19

Day 1
2. a
3. Answers will vary.

Day 2
2. d
3. b
4. Answers will vary.

Day 3
2. c
3. b

Day 4
2. c
3. a

Day 5
1. D   2. G   3. D   4. H

Week 20

Day 1
2. c
3. a

Day 2
2. b
3. d

Day 3
2. a
3. c

Day 4
2. b
3. a

Day 5
1. D   2. G   3. C   4. F

Week 21

Day 1
2. d
3. c
4. Answers will vary.

Day 2
2. a
3. b

Day 3
2. c
3. d

Day 4
2. b
3. a
4. Answers will vary.

Day 5
1. C   2. J   3. A   4. G

Week 22

Day 1
2. c
3. a

Day 2
2. b
3. d

Day 3
2. a
3. b

Day 4
2. d
3. c
4. Answers will vary.

Day 5
1. D   2. F   3. B   4. F

Week 23

Day 1
2. b
3. d

Day 2
2. c
3. b

Day 3
2. b
3. a

Day 4

2. d

3. c

4. Answers will vary.

Day 5

1. C 2. F 3. B 4. J

Week 24

Day 1

2. c

3. b

Day 2

2. d

3. a

Day 3

2. a

3. c

Day 4

2. d

3. b

4. Answers will vary.

Day 5

1. D 2. G 3. A 4. H

Week 25

Day 1

2. a

3. b

4. Answers will vary.

Day 2

2. b

3. c

Day 3

2. d

3. b

Day 4

2. c

3. c

4. Answers will vary.

Day 5

1. D 2. G 3. D 4. F

Week 26

Day 1

2. d

3. c

Day 2

2. b

3. c

4. Answers will vary.

Day 3

2. d

3. b

Day 4

2. a

3. d

4. Answers will vary.

Day 5

1. C 2. G 3. B 4. J

Week 27 Review

Day 1

comparable, Preceding, distinction, approximately, compact

Day 2

distinguish, concise, formulated, cohesive, initiated

Day 3

debates, Prior, issues, construct, absolute

Day 4

foresee, condense, initial, delete, inserted, anticipation

Day 5

Across

1. approximate
8. expectation
9. precede
10. insertion

Down

1. anticipate
2. absolutely
3. deletion
4. discriminate
5. condensed
6. constructive
7. subsequent

Week 28

Day 1

2. c

3. d

4. Answers will vary.

Day 2

2. c

3. b

Day 3

2. a

3. d

Day 4

2. b

3. d

4. Answers will vary.

Day 5

1. A 2. H 3. B 4. J

Week 29

Day 1

2. b

3. c

4. Answers will vary.

Day 2

2. d

3. d

Day 3

2. a

3. b

Day 4

2. c

3. a, d

4. Answers will vary.

Day 5

1. B 2. F 3. D 4. G

Week 30

Day 1

2. d

3. b

4. Answers will vary.

Day 2

2. c

3. d

Day 3

2. a

3. b

4. Answers will vary.

Day 4

2. c

3. explains how things fly

Day 5

1. C 2. J 3. B 4. F

Week 31

Day 1
2. c
3. a

Day 2
2. a
3. b
4. Answers will vary.

Day 3
2. a, c
3. c

Day 4
2. a
3. b
4. Answers will vary.

Day 5
1. B   2. F   3. D   4. G

Week 32

Day 1
2. d
3. b

Day 2
2. b
3. d

Day 3
2. a
3. b
4. Answers will vary.

Day 4
2. a, d
3. b

Day 5
1. D   2. H   3. B   4. H

Week 33

Day 1
2. a
3. c

Day 2
2. d
3. Answers will vary.

Day 3
2. c
3. d
4. Answers will vary.

Day 4
2. a
3. c

Day 5
1. D   2. G   3. A   4. G

Week 34

Day 1
2. b
3. d
4. Answers will vary.

Day 2
2. c, d
3. b

Day 3
2. c
3. a
4. Answers will vary.

Day 4
2. a
3. c

Day 5
1. C   2. G   3. A   4. H

Week 35

Day 1
2. b
3. d

Day 2
2. c
3. a

Day 3
2. b
3. d

Day 4
2. a
3. c
4. Answers will vary.

Day 5
1. B   2. F   3. D   4. F

Week 36 Review

Day 1
feasible, inherent, persistent, connotation

Day 2
relevant, speculate, hypothesis, asserted, integrated, continuous, occasionally

Day 3
probable, integral, appropriate, speculation, subjective

Day 4
explicit, potential, implicit, objective, pertinent

Day 5
1. intermittent
2. occasional
3. plausible
4. cite
5. pertain
6. denotation
7. validate
8. bias
code: "Because it is there."

    Daily Academic Vocabulary • EMC 2762 • © Evan-Moor Corp.

Index

absolute 82, 114
absolutely 82, 114
account 66, 78
account for 66, 78
accumulate 74, 78
accumulation 74, 78
acquire 74, 78
analysis 70, 78
analyze 70, 78
anticipate 98, 114
anticipation 98, 114
appropriate 146, 150
approximate 82, 114
approximately 82, 114
assert 138, 150
bias 122, 150
biased 122, 150
character 34, 42
characteristic 34, 42
characterize 34, 42
citation 138, 150
cite 138, 150
classification 70, 78
classify 70, 78
cohesive 90, 114
compact 90, 114
comparable 82, 114
compile 74, 78
conceive 10, 42
concept 10, 42
conceptualize 10, 42
concise 90, 114
condense 90, 114
condensed 90, 114
connotation 142, 150
construct 110, 114
constructive 110, 114
contemplate 46, 78
continuous 130, 150
debate 86, 114
delete 94, 114
deletion 94, 114
demonstrate 30, 42

demonstration 30, 42
denotation 142, 150
discriminate 106, 114
dissimilar 22, 42
distinction 106, 114
distinguish 106, 114
equivalent 22, 42
essential 38, 42
establish 30, 42
exaggerate 18, 42
exaggeration 18, 42
exclude 50, 78
expectation 98, 114
explicit 142, 150
feasible 134, 150
foresee 98, 114
former 54, 78
formulate 110, 114
hypothesis 126, 150
hypothesize 126, 150
identical 22, 42
implicit 142, 150
inconceivable 10, 42
infer 46, 78
inference 46, 78
inherent 118, 150
initial 110, 114
initiate 110, 114
insert 94, 114
insertion 94, 114
integral 118, 150
integrate 118, 150
integration 118, 150
intend 14, 42
intention 14, 42
intermittent 130, 150
involve 50, 78
irrelevant 146, 150
issue 86, 114
latter 54, 78
manner 58, 78
method 62, 78
minimal 18, 42

minimize 18, 42
minimum 18, 42
narrate 26, 42
narration 26, 42
narrative 26, 42
narrator 26, 42
objective 122, 150
occasional 130, 150
occasionally 130, 150
omission 50, 78
omit 50, 78
option 38, 42
optional 38, 42
persistent 130, 150
pertain 146, 150
pertinent 146, 150
plausible 134, 150
potential 134, 150
precede 102, 114
preceding 102, 114
prior 102, 114
probable 134, 150
procedure 62, 78
property 34, 42
proposal 14, 42
propose 14, 42
proposition 14, 42
relevant 146, 150
speculate 126, 150
speculation 126, 150
strategize 62, 78
strategy 62, 78
subjective 122, 150
subsequent 102, 114
surmise 46, 78
system 58, 78
systematic 58, 78
theory 126, 150
trait 34, 42
unique 22, 42
validate 138, 150
version 66, 78
vital 38, 42

conceive

(verb)   To think up or form in the mind.

*Kari will **conceive** a plan to raise money for the new theater.*

inconceivable

(adj.)   Impossible to believe or imagine.

*It was **inconceivable** to me that Luis would not tell the truth.*

concept

(noun)   A general idea or thought.

*Fairness is a **concept** that most people understand.*

conceptualize

(verb)   To form a concept or idea.

*When inventors **conceptualize** solutions to problems, they create new inventions.*

propose • proposal | DAY 1

propose

| (verb) | To suggest a plan or idea to be considered. | *Each member will **propose** a topic for the group project.* |

---

proposal

| (noun) | A suggestion or plan. | *The group wrote a **proposal** to take a field trip.* |

proposition | DAY 2

| (noun) | An offered or suggested plan of action. | *Enrique's **proposition** was that he would mow her lawn for a small fee.* |

intend | DAY 3

| (verb) | To have something in mind as a goal, plan, or purpose. | *The students **intend** to raise money to pay for a class trip.* |

intention | DAY 4

| (noun) | Something that you mean to do. | *The team's **intention** is to win the final game.* |

exaggerate • exaggeration

exaggerate

(verb) To make something seem larger, more valuable, or more important than it is.

*Drawings sometimes **exaggerate** the size of a shark's teeth.*

exaggeration

(noun) The act of exaggerating.

*It is an **exaggeration** to say that I can hit a ball clear into the next county.*

minimize

(verb) To make something as small as possible.

*We can **minimize** the amount of work for each student if we work together as a team.*

minimum

(noun) The smallest possible amount or lowest limit.

*One dollar is the **minimum** that you can donate to the fund.*

minimal

(adj.) Being the smallest in amount or size.

*It takes **minimal** effort to smile, but the rewards are big.*

unique

(adj.) Being the only one of its kind.

*The painting is **unique** because it is the only one by this artist.*

identical

(adj.) Exactly alike.

*No two days in school are **identical** because something different happens each day.*

dissimilar

(adj.) Not alike; different.

*Even though they are twins, the girls are **dissimilar**.*

equivalent

(adj.) The same as, or equal to, another thing.

*The winter break from school is shorter than summer vacation. They are not **equivalent**.*

narrate

(verb) To tell the story or give an account of something in speech or writing.

*Each team member will **narrate** a portion of the presentation.*

narrator

(noun) A person or character who tells a story.

*The play has a **narrator** who introduces all the characters.*

narrative

(noun) A story, description, or account of events.

*The assignment was to write a **narrative** about your first day of school.*

narration

(noun) The act of narrating.

*The concert will include music and **narration** about the history of our country.*

demonstrate • demonstration

demonstrate

(verb) To teach or explain by showing how to do or use something.

*The coach will **demonstrate** the proper way to hold a bat.*

demonstration

(noun) An act of teaching, explaining, or operating something.

*The health class will get a **demonstration** of how to clean a cut.*

demonstrate

(verb) To prove or show clearly.

*A capable lawyer will **demonstrate** her client's innocence.*

establish

(verb) To prove or show something to be true.

*The attendance count will **establish** that most students in our school are present today.*

establish

(verb) To create or start.

*The school will **establish** a new award to recognize good conduct.*

Daily Academic Vocabulary

trait

(noun) A special quality or feature of a person or animal.

*Creativity is a **trait** that most artists have.*

characteristic • character

characteristic

(noun) A regular quality or feature of someone or something.

*Fast action is a **characteristic** of a soccer game.*

character

(noun) All of the many things that make one person or thing different from another.

*The parks and playgrounds in this neighborhood give it a friendly **character**.*

characterize

(verb) To describe the character and qualities of someone or something.

*You could **characterize** life in a city as noisy and busy.*

property

(noun) A distinctive physical characteristic of something; a common quality of all things belonging to a particular group.

*One **property** of oxygen is that it has no smell.*

option

(noun) One of several things that can be chosen.

*Pizza is one **option** for lunch today.*

optional

(adj.) Left to your own choice to do; not required.

*Attending school is not **optional** for most students.*

essential

(adj.) Very important or necessary.

*Learning to read is an **essential** skill.*

(noun) A necessary thing to have.

*One **essential** for learning to read is a book.*

vital

(adj.) Very important or essential.

*Getting enough calcium is **vital** for strong bones.*

infer

(verb) To draw a conclusion after considering specific evidence or facts.

*Students can **infer** from the materials on their desks that they are doing an experiment today.*

inference

(noun) A conclusion drawn by reasoning from facts and evidence.

*When Sean didn't attend the audition, we made the **inference** that he didn't want to be in the play.*

surmise

(verb) To draw a conclusion without certain knowledge; suppose.

*I **surmise** that we will go on vacation this year, but my parents haven't said anything yet.*

contemplate

(verb) To think about deeply and seriously.

*The teacher will **contemplate** the students' suggestions.*

Daily Academic Vocabulary • EMC 2762 • © Evan-Moor Corp.

involve

(verb) To have something as a necessary part; include.

*Winning the championship will **involve** beating every team.*

involve • exclude

involve

(verb) To bring into a situation.

*Our teacher **involves** parents as guest speakers on Occupation Day.*

exclude

(verb) To keep or leave something or someone out.

*We **exclude** some jobs on Occupation Day because we can't include everything.*

omit

(verb) To leave out; not include.

*Let's not **omit** a single event when we describe our fantastic vacation!*

omission

(noun) Something that is left out, removed, or not done.

*It was an **omission** to not give credit to everyone who worked on the project.*

former
DAY 1

(noun) The first of two things mentioned.

*Between the first-grade teacher and the fifth-grade teacher, the **former** has been teaching longer.*

former
DAY 2

(adj.) Having to do with the past; previous.

*The **former** principal of our school returned to receive an award.*

latter
DAY 3

(noun) The second of two things mentioned.

*We will visit a museum and an aquarium, but we are more excited about the **latter** because we love fish!*

latter
DAY 4

(adj.) Near the end.

*The **latter** part of the book, after the hero is captured, is the most exciting to read.*

Daily Academic Vocabulary • EMC 2762 • © Evan-Moor Corp.

manner

(noun) A way of doing things; style.

*The careful **manner** in which Harris always completes his homework impresses his teacher.*

system

(noun) A group of related things or parts that work together as a whole.

*The computer **system** stopped working when the electricity went off.*

system

(noun) A particular way or method of doing something.

*Arianna needs a better **system** for remembering her homework, because she often forgets to bring it to school.*

systematic

(adj.) Involving or based on a method or plan.

*A more **systematic** way to organize our class library would be to arrange the books by subject matter.*

strategy

(noun) A careful plan or method for achieving a goal.

*The student's **strategy** for winning the reading contest is to read a book every day.*

strategize

(verb) To plan or decide on a strategy.

*Our science team **strategized** on how to finish our project on time.*

procedure

(noun) A way of doing something following an orderly series of steps.

*The students learned the fire-safety **procedure** of stop, drop, and roll.*

method

(noun) A way in which something is done.

*One **method** of learning the words is to make flashcards.*

account

(noun) A written or spoken description of something that has happened.

*Each student will give an **account** of the class field trip.*

account for

(verb) To explain.

*We can **account for** the missing equipment, which was loaned to another team.*

version

(noun) A description or account from a particular point of view.

*Each child had a different **version** of how the window was broken.*

version

(noun) A changed or different form of something.

*Adam chose to include a pink rose instead of a red rose in his **version** of the flower painting.*

analyze

(verb) To examine something in great detail in order to understand it.

*The teacher will **analyze** the test results to determine what skills students need help on.*

analysis

(noun) A careful study of the parts of something in order to better understand the whole.

*The principal's **analysis** of the new rules showed that they help students get along better.*

classify

(verb) To put things into groups based on their characteristics.

*We can **classify** our family's pets into two groups— those with fur and those with feathers.*

classification

(noun) An arrangement of things into groups based on their characteristics.

*One simple **classification** of books is fiction and nonfiction.*

        Daily Academic Vocabulary • EMC 2762 • © Evan-Moor Corp.

acquire

(verb) To get as your own. *I just **acquired** a new bike.*

accumulate

(verb) To collect, gather together, or let pile up. *I will **accumulate** many rocks in order to build a wall.*

accumulation

(noun) An amount that collects or piles up. *There is an **accumulation** of empty bottles in the garage.*

compile

(verb) To collect or put together in an orderly form. *We should **compile** the list of sources that we used for our report.*

approximate

(adj.) More or less accurate or correct.

*We only need to report the **approximate** length of the hallway.*

approximately

(adv.) Not exactly, but nearly.

*We have **approximately** one hour to work on the project.*

comparable

(adj.) Nearly the same; similar.

*Both pairs of sneakers are **comparable** in price.*

absolute • absolutely

absolute

(adj.) Complete; total; without limit.

*I have **absolute** confidence in my ability to do this activity.*

absolutely

(adv.) Completely; totally.

*I checked my work, and I am **absolutely** sure it is correct.*

Daily Academic Vocabulary • EMC 2762 • © Evan-Moor Corp.

debate

(verb)	To discuss the arguments for or against something.	*Our class will **debate** another class about the choice of school mascot.*
(noun)	A discussion of arguments for or against something.	*There was a **debate** between two classes over the choice of school mascot.*

debate

(verb)	To think over carefully before making a decision.	*I **debated** whether to play in the band or sing in the chorus.*

issue

(noun)	A subject of debate or argument.	*The classes discussed the **issue** of student rights.*

issue

(verb)	To send or give out something.	*The principal will **issue** a statement that recognizes students for their participation in the recycling program.*

concise

| (adj.) | Saying a lot in a few words. | *A dictionary gives a **concise** definition of each word.* |

compact

| (adj.) | Not taking up too much space. | *We have small lockers so our belongings have to be **compact**.* |

condensed • condense

condensed

| (adj.) | Shortened or made smaller. | *A **condensed** story has the less important parts cut out.* |

condense

| (verb) | To make smaller or shorter. | *You must **condense** the report to fit on only one page.* |

cohesive

| (adj.) | Holding or working together as a whole. | *A **cohesive** team cooperates to get a job done.* |

insert • insertion

insert

(verb) To put or place inside something.

*You should **insert** a comma between the city and state.*

insertion

(noun) The act of inserting.

*The **insertion** of a comma will correct the error.*

insertion

(noun) Something, such as a word or phrase, that has been inserted.

*A comma was the only **insertion** that was needed in your entire report.*

delete • deletion

delete

(verb) To remove from a piece of writing or computer text.

*Please **delete** the period and add a question mark.*

deletion

(noun) The act of deleting.

*The **deletion** of a period takes one touch of a computer key.*

deletion

(noun) Something, such as a word or phrase, that has been deleted.

*You made the wrong **deletion** and now the sentence doesn't make sense.*

foresee

(verb) To see or realize in advance that something will happen.

*The teacher could **foresee** that the students who followed the directions carefully would produce a better project.*

anticipate • anticipation

anticipate

(verb) To expect.

*The students **anticipate** the usual Friday quiz.*

anticipation

(noun) The act or process of anticipating.

*In **anticipation** of the Friday quiz, most students reviewed their notes on Thursday.*

expectation

(noun) The feeling or belief that something is likely to happen.

*It is our **expectation** that we will have fun on the field trip.*

expectation

(noun) A standard of conduct or performance expected.

*The student lived up to the **expectations** of her teacher by passing the test.*

Daily Academic Vocabulary • EMC 2762 • © Evan-Moor Corp.

subsequent

(adj.) Coming after in time or order.

*If we lose this round, we will need to win the **subsequent** round to stay in the tournament.*

precede

(verb) To come before in time.

*For many children, a year of preschool **precedes** kindergarten.*

preceding

(adj.) Coming just before.

*The sky grew very dark in the moments **preceding** the storm.*

prior

(adj.) Earlier in time or coming before.

*We build on **prior** knowledge to learn something new.*

distinguish

(verb) To tell apart by knowing or seeing the difference between two things.

*We **distinguish** between the two students by their hair color.*

distinguish

(verb) To see or hear clearly.

*I could not **distinguish** her voice on the phone because she was whispering.*

discriminate

(verb) To see a clear difference between things, people, or behavior.

*A chef can **discriminate** between the flavors in foods.*

distinction

(noun) A feature that makes someone or something different.

*Even though they are twins, there are definite **distinctions** in their personalities.*

construct

| (verb) | To build or put together. | *We **constructed** a model of the solar system from styrofoam and hangers.* |

constructive

| (adj.) | Serving a useful purpose; helpful. | *His **constructive** comment helped me find a solution to my problem.* |

formulate

| (verb) | To work out an idea or opinion or to state something carefully and precisely. | *We will **formulate** a persuasive plan to get permission for a field trip.* |

initiate • initial

initiate

| (verb) | To start; to cause to begin. | *The warring countries will **initiate** peace talks.* |

initial

| (adj.) | First, or at the beginning. | *Our **initial** plan was to see a movie, but we went hiking instead.* |

integrate
DAY 1

(verb) To combine things and make into a whole.

*I will **integrate** many subplots into my story.*

integration
DAY 2

(noun) The act of combining all parts into a whole.

*The **integration** of their group into ours will create one very strong team.*

integral
DAY 3

(adj.) Forming an essential part of something.

*Teamwork is an **integral** part of any group project.*

inherent
DAY 4

(adj.) Being a core or inborn characteristic of something.

*The student's **inherent** loyalty made him a good friend.*

objective

(adj.) Based on fact, not feelings or opinions.

*The judges were **objective** and chose the winner based on the quality of the entry.*

subjective

(adj.) Based on feelings or opinions rather than on fact.

*The judges were **subjective** and only looked at the entries they liked.*

bias

(noun) A strong feeling for or against something that does not let someone be fair.

*The contest shows a **bias** for students who have talent in music or art.*

biased

(adj.) Favoring or opposing one person, group, or point of view more than others.

*The students were **biased** and believed their team was the best.*

speculate

(verb)	To wonder or guess about something without knowing all the facts.	*I can only **speculate** on my grade until I get my score.*

speculation

(noun)	A conclusion that is reached by wondering and guessing without all the facts.	*There is **speculation** about who will be chosen for the team.*

hypothesize • hypothesis

hypothesize

(verb)	To make a guess based on some knowledge.	*We can **hypothesize** that the rock will fall faster than the feather.*

hypothesis

(noun)	A prediction or guess based on some knowledge.	*Our **hypothesis** is that the rock will fall faster than the feather.*

theory

(noun)	A proposed explanation of something.	*The global warming **theory** explains how the Earth's temperature is rising.*

occasional • occasionally   DAY 1

occasional

| (adj.) | Happening from time to time. | *We have an **occasional** assembly at school.* |

occasionally

| (adv.) | From time to time. | *We **occasionally** get to hear the chorus and band perform.* |

intermittent   DAY 2

| (adj.) | Starting and stopping; not happening at regular times. | *The school has visiting authors who work with students on an **intermittent** basis.* |

continuous   DAY 3

| (adj.) | Going on without stopping. | *Many people believe that learning should be **continuous** all through life.* |

persistent   DAY 4

| (adj.) | Lasting for a long time. | *There is a **persistent** smell in the science lab that should be checked.* |

| (adj.) | Refusing to give up or let go despite many challenges. | *He is **persistent** and determined to succeed.* |

probable

(adj.)	Likely to happen or be true.	*The **probable** outcome of the race will be a win for our team.*

plausible

(adj.)	Believable; likely, but not certain, to be true.	*She gave a **plausible** excuse for not attending the ceremony.*

feasible

(adj.)	Capable of being done or brought about.	*Finishing the project this week is a **feasible** objective.*

potential

(adj.)	Able to come into being; possible.	*The negotiators tried to avoid **potential** conflict between the two countries.*

cite

(verb) To refer to for explanation or proof.

*I always **cite** the sources that I use in my reports.*

citation

(noun) A short note recognizing a source of information or of a quoted passage.

*The **citation** of the history book informed the reader where the writer found her information.*

assert

(verb) To state or declare strongly.

*We need to **assert** our support of our friend.*

validate

(verb) To prove true or factual; to confirm by giving evidence or support.

*The research I found **validates** my idea.*

explicit
DAY 1

(adj.)	Very clearly stated; precise.	*We received **explicit** instructions for the assignment.*

implicit
DAY 2

(adj.)	Not stated but understood in what is said; implied.	*It was **implicit** from the instructions that the assignment was important and should be done carefully.*

denotation
DAY 3

(noun)	The most specific, exact meaning of a word or expression.	*The **denotation** of the word "school" is a place where students are taught.*

connotation
DAY 4

(noun)	An additional meaning associated with or suggested by a word besides the exact meaning.	*For many students, the **connotation** of "school" is the place where they see their friends.*

relevant • irrelevant
DAY 1

relevant

(adj.) Having to do with what is currently being discussed or is important.

*Knowing the last day of school is **relevant** to making our summer vacation plans.*

---

irrelevant

(adj.) Not having to do with what is being considered or discussed.

*The date of winter break is **irrelevant** to making our summer plans.*

appropriate
DAY 2

(adj.) Suitable, or right for the purpose.

*It is **appropriate** that all students who made an extra effort should receive an award.*

pertain
DAY 3

(verb) To relate to or have to do with something.

*Those materials all **pertain** to geometry.*

pertinent
DAY 4

(adj.) Having to do with or connected to a subject.

*That book is **pertinent** to our discussion of books to read this summer.*